THE DAGGER OF ISLAM

Within Islam, the "dagger"—in the form of machine gun, bomb and hangman's rope— is well-bloodied. Men —and sometimes women—are struck down with a frequency and ferocity which is only dimly perceived in the Western world. Assassination is an accepted means of political expression. Between 1948 and 1979, 25 heads of state and prime ministers were murdered as were another 20 ex-prime ministers or senior ex-ministers. One was killed in London. Numerous unsuccessful murder attempts were made on the lives of other leaders —including fourteen known attempts to kill King Hussein of Jordan.

Plots and counterplots abound in Islam. The first phase of the Iranian revolution was scarcely over before emissaries of Khomeini were visiting Damascus to discuss ways of cooperating with the Syrians at the expense of Iraq, despite the fact that Syria and Iraq have declared themselves a "union."

Khomeini wished to weaken Iraq, a traditional rival of Iran, from within ...

THE DAGGER
OF ISLAM

John Laffin

BANTAM BOOKS
TORONTO • NEW YORK • LONDON

THE DAGGER OF ISLAM
*A Bantam Book / published by arrangement with
Sphere Books Limited*

PRINTING HISTORY
*First published by Sphere Books Ltd. 1979
Revised Bantam edition / March 1981*

ISBN 0–553–14287–9

Published simultaneously in the United States and Canada

*Bantam Books are published by Bantam Books, Inc. Its trade-
mark, consisting of the words "Bantam Books" and the por-
trayal of a bantam, is Registered in U.S. Patent and Trademark
Office and in other countries. Marca Registrada. Bantam
Books, Inc., 666 Fifth Avenue, New York, New York 10103.*

PRINTED IN THE UNITED STATES OF AMERICA

0 9 8 7 6 5 4 3 2 1

CONTENTS

1

WARNINGS

There is genuine fear that Muslims may be creating a great deal of trouble for themselves and the rest of the world by unleashing forces which they may not be able to control or direct.

> Altaf Gauhar, in *The Guardian*, London,
> February 26, 1979

We are at war. And our battle has only just begun. Our first victory will be one tract of land somewhere in the world that is under the complete rule of Islam . . . Islam is moving across the earth . . . Nothing can stop [it] spreading in Europe and America.

> 'Abd al-Qadir as-Sufi ad-Darqawi,
> in *Jihad—a Ground Plan*, published in Britain by
> Diwan Press, 1978

As a creed with which Europe and America has to do business, Islam has begun to make Marxism look decidedly familiar and manageable . . . It presents itself as a powerful third force in international affairs.

> *Guardian Weekly* editorial,
> London
> April 14, 1979

Historically, Islam has made good its capacity to belong with wide diversities of humankind. But always,

1

traditionally, this universality was on the basis of surrender.

Kenneth Cragg, *The House of Islam*,
2nd edition, Dickenson Publishing Co., California, 1978

The sudden injection of Islam as a third force hostile to both the Christian West and the communist bloc has overturned some carefully nurtured assumptions held by many an observer of world events.

Mowahid H. Shah, *Christian Science Monitor*,
January 28, 1980

The Muslims are coming, despite Jewish cunning, Christian hatred and the Communist storm.

The Cairo Muslim magazine *Al Da'wah* (The Call)
March 21, 1979

Islam is once again on the march out of Arabia; it is a Muslim crusade, a religious and cultural jihad or holy war ... Who knows what djinna [the Islamic resurgence] has let loose upon the world?

Christopher Dobson and Ronald Payne,
The Sunday Telegraph, London,
March 25, 1979

A wave of religious fanaticism is sweeping the Arab world—indeed the whole Muslim world—and the consequences could be revolutionary.

An editorial in *To the Point International*, Antwerp,
November 14, 1977

The spread of Islam was military. There is a tendency to apologize for this and we should not. It is one of the injunctions of the Koran that you must fight for the spreading of Islam.

Dr. Ali Issa Othman, for some years adviser to UNRWA
on education; quoted by Charis Waddy in
The Muslim Mind, Longmans, London, 1976

The 'ulama [the "learned" doctors of Islam] by encouraging a violent and fanatical spirit have given Muhammadanism a sinister reputation contrary to many precepts of its founder.

Alfred Guillaume, *Islam,* Penguin 1978 edition

As reports of Islamic revival sweep from Africa to Southeast Asia, it behooves the adherents of other faiths, or no faith, to try to understand the religious strivings of so many millions of their fellow human beings ... There is a previously under-estimated force at work.

An editorial in *Christian Science Monitor,*
February 19, 1979

When my mind travels to the eighty million Muslims of Indonesia, the fifty million in China, and the several other millions in Malaya, Siam and Burma, and the hundred million in Pakistan, the hundred or more in the Middle East and the forty million in Russia, as well as the other millions in the distant parts of the world, when I visualize these millions united in one faith, I have a great consciousness of the tremendous potentialities that cooperation among them can achieve.

Gamal Abdel Nasser, late President of Egypt,
in *The Philosophy of the Revolution,* 1955

Our frontiers are not our limits but our wounds.

Shukri al-Quwaitli, one time President of Syria

The Islamic religion is based on the pursuit of domination and power and strength and might.

Mumammad al-Mutti Bakhit, in
Haquiaat al-Islam, Cairo, 1926.

2

A GREAT ANGUISH
AN ARC OF CRISIS

Outside al Azhar, the great Islamic university and religious center in Cairo, is a large illuminated billboard proclaiming 1,000 MILLION MUSLIMS. It is not only a bold sign but a significant one, for Islam does not yet have this many adherents. The current figure is about 900 million* and the 1,000 million is the target for the year AD 2000.

The billboard and the number indicate Islamic ambition and they hint at a surging power which goes far beyond mere numbers. After all, the Christian world has 985 million people, but this does not mean that Christianity is stronger than Islam. Christianity is nothing more than a vein to Islam's artery. Islam is not, as in Christianity, a church within the community, but a community integrated with religion and in this lies its special strength.

The average Western person does not realize that Islam is not merely religious but political, economic and legal as well, an all-embracing system, code and pattern of life,

*An accurate figure is impossible to reach. *Encyclopaedia Britannica* puts the number at 536 million; various Islamic and Arabic authorities say between 600 and 900 million. Mr. Ahmed Heiba, an agricultural consultant with the Islamic Development Bank, suggests 800 million. The 1977 edition of the *World Muslim Gazetteer*, published by the World Muslim Congress in Karachi, gives a world total of over 900,000,000 (from 647,000,000 in the 1964 edition).

4

not just something to which Muslims turn on Friday, their principal day of prayer.

That something is stirring in Islam is apparent from even a cursory glance at newspapers. The words Islam and Muslim have appeared in headlines over stories concerned with revolution and executions in Iran, the judicial murder of ex-President Bhutto of Pakistan, the stoning to death of adulterers in Saudi Arabia, the use of the so-called "oil weapon," the Palestinian homeland issue, the storming of foreign embassies, and the holding of diplomat hostages at the American embassy in Teheran.

Despite the coverage of the Islamic world by the media generally, the West—indeed the whole of the non-Muslim world—is startlingly ignorant of Islam. Among private individuals this lack of information is probably nothing more than unfortunate but the ignorance extends to the leaders of the Western, Communist and Third Worlds, and this is dangerous. It can also be fatal. On the international scene, American ignorance about Islam in Iran led to one of the greatest setbacks ever to American prestige. Individuals can also suffer through the ignorance of third parties. For instance, the well-intentioned appeals by world political and religious leaders made to President Zia al-Huq to spare Mr. Bhutto's life ensured only that he had no chance at all. It is true that he never did have much chance—the laws of an Islamic republic being what they are—but "interference" from outside effectively did away with whatever slight chance remained.

All the events reported from the Islamic world indicate that "one of the world's great religions is in the throes of a great anguish," as a *Christian Science Monitor* journalist, Geoffrey Goodsell, has described it.

Zbigniew Brzezinski, U.S. presidential adviser on national security, places this anguish in its political context. "An arc of crisis stretches along the shores of the Indian Ocean, with fragile social and political structures in a region of vital importance to us threatened by fragmentation. The resulting political chaos could well be filled by elements hostile to our values and sympathetic to our adversaries."

Dr. Brzezinski's "arc of crisis" extends from Iran to

Southeast Asia, taking in Afghanistan, the Gulf States, Pakistan, Bangladesh, the Yemens and Somalia, all Islamic states. But the area of *potential* crisis is much more extensive, stretching from Morocco to Egypt and including much of North Africa; it involves Turkey and the six Muslim states of the Soviet Union; it reaches as far as Indonesia and the Philippines. It covers the forty-four states of the Muslim world, and of the Islamic Union which today has sizeable minority populations in the West—a million in Britain and two million in France, for example. Overall, Islam represents a medium-term change in the world balance of power. At the UN or at any of the great world conferences almost a quarter of the delegates are likely to have a background of the Muslim faith.

Criticism of Islam from within is rare—and dangerous; Miss M'rabet made her comments from the safety of France. By its very nature as much as by religious exhortation Islam is closed against criticism—even of the most academic, constructive nature—by its followers. Some of those who have broken the rules have suffered grievously, as this book will show. Most writers about Islam are European and American—sociologists, historians, psychologists, political scientists, journalists. At any level the outsider is more likely to see what is happening to Islam because within Islam so much is covered up and distorted in efforts to save face within the Islamic community.

My purpose in writing this book is to inform, to warn and to express compassion. Compassion is certainly desirable as the great mass of Muslims are being swept helplessly along by a turbulent wind of political-social-religious reaction beyond their power to check. Indeed the so-called Islamic resurgence is possibly the most widespread and profound reactionary movement in political history. Not since the fierce warrior tribes of Believers— the followers of the Prophet Muhammad—swept out of the deserts of the Arabian Peninsula in the seventh century to establish an empire which occupied much of the world and threatened the rest of it, has Islam felt so strong and confident.

The Muslim revival does not mean, yet, a great move

towards Muslim solidarity or Muslim unity in the political sense. Islam is split by religious crevasses as deep and dangerous as those which split Europe at the time of Luther or the Anabaptists. The divisions would be even more intense and bitter if the Arab-Israeli dispute did not exist. This conflict preoccupies a lot of militant Muslims who would otherwise be fighting among themselves.

Few great problems of the world can be solved without an understanding of how Islam works. Fully to comprehend Islam it is first necessary to understand its rigidity— a word I use here in no pejorative sense.* It is rigid because it is traditional, because it is an imperative system of belief and because it sees itself as a religion perfected. The Islamic belief in Allah (God) is real and vital, with a power to dictate thought and action that the West can no longer sense. Muslims, more than Christians and Jews, are committed to the establishment of the Kingdom of God on earth. Religious laws insist that the words *in sha'Allah* must precede all actions—"If God wills." Looking back, it is hardly surprising that a desert people, facing potential disaster throughout life in their harsh environment should believe in an inexorable fate that man cannot control. This became "The Will of Allah."

Rigidity forces Islam to reject most "isms," an attitude which is understandable enough when they concern political or economic attitudes, but it also rejects evolution *as a scientific study*. While a good many Muslim scholars educated in the West accept it, many others oppose it because it is in direct conflict with the Koran. In this they are like those Christians who take the Bible so literally that they can tolerate no other point of view. It is disturbing to find an Iranian scholar of Professor Seyyed Nasr's erudition proclaiming that "the Darwinian theory of evolution . . . is metaphysically impossible and logically absurd." Such a rigid frame of mind is virtually impossible to argue with, even in an academic way. It sweeps away

*Unfortunately Muslims will take it pejoratively. Many generations of non-Muslim "orientalists" (an old-fashioned term), "Arabists" and Islamic scholars have learned, to their disappointment, that opinion which does not conform to the Islam self-image is resented.

all the evidence of anthropology, archaeology, biology, geomorphology and the most advanced medical-scientific evidence. The Koran does not acknowledge the possibility of evolution so it does not exist. If this opinion were reached as the result of examining the evidence we could accept it—but it is reached by *not* examining the evidence, by refusing to admit the possibility of evolutionary evidence.

Despite this disinclination for pure research the Muslim intelligentsia and the Muslim theocracy believe that in Islam they have the cure for the Western world's maladies —and they are not too happy about the patient having a choice on whether or not he takes the medicine. As Albert Hourani has so ironically put it, "Muslims believed themselves obliged to keep their neighbors' consciences as well as their own."* Kenneth Cragg is more explicit. "The role of Islam in relation to all other religions is to prune, correct, purge and complete them."†

If Islam's conduct were limited to its religious activity, no matter how patronizing, it might be tolerated. But, as I must stress again, Islam is not only a religion and even to speak of the "religious side" of Islam is to perform an impossible amputation. Islam is all-round, a whole, a force which moves all its elements at the same time; it is theology as law. And it is this relentless and remorseless nature which should concern us in the West.

For the Muslim, religion has to do with action rather than analysis; there is no place for abstract thought, for the "contemplation" which is so strong a part of the Christian faith.

Writing in the *Sunday Telegraph* on December 17, 1978, Peregrine Worsthorne summed up the dangers in his usual uncomfortable and uncompromising way. "To encourage resurgent Islam to assume that it can get away with what amounts to a new-style jihad, without its militancy being met by ours, this would be to condemn Christendom to an ignoble fate, as much invited as deserved."

*Arabic Thought in the Liberal Age 1798–1939, Oxford University Press, 1970.
†The House of Islam, Dickenson Publishing Co., 1975.

But we cannot begin to discuss Islam let alone confront it unless we examine its origins, founder, and its Holy Book, its law, customs and traditions, its attitude to women and minorities, its leaders and literature, what it claims to be and what it proves itself to be.

3

"HISTORY SURRENDERED TO OUR WILL"

Islam was founded—Muslims would say "revealed"—by Muhammad, who was born about AD 570 to a member of the respected Meccan clan of Hashim. Some followers later claimed that at Muhammad's birth the palace of the Persian emperor trembled and that a mysterious light ignited at his mother's breast, shining all the way to Syria, 800 miles away. It was said that Muhammad's body cast no shadow and that when his hair fell into a fire it would not burn. Muhammad made no such claims, insisting that he was merely the link of communication between God and man.

His father died shortly before Muhammad's birth and his mother when he was six. Two years later his grandfather, Abd al-Muttalib, died, leaving the boy in the care of a poor uncle, Abu Talib. As a youth Muhammad was set to work tending his uncle's camels, a task recalled in adulthood as a mark of divine favor. "Allah sent no prophet who was not a herdsman," he told his disciples.

As a young man Muhammad was exposed to the stimulus of religious debate then common in the Middle East. He listened avidly as Jews and Christians argued over their faiths and these discussions may have deepened his dissatisfaction with the traditional Arab polytheistic religion with its array of tribal gods and jinn.

At twenty-five Muhammad accepted a marriage proposal from Khadijah, a rich Meccan widow fifteen years his senior, for whom he had already led a successful caravan. With his financial security assured by Khadijah's wealth and business, he began to venture alone into the desert, to contemplate and pray.

According to legend, Muhammad, though illiterate, had earned a reputation as a wise and saintly man long before his first revelation from the Angel Gabriel. Looking from the balcony of his Mecca home one day he saw the members of four clans arguing over which of them should be allowed the honor of carrying the Black Stone, a large meteorite that the Arabs regarded as sacred, to its new resting place in a rebuilt shrine, now famous as the Ka'ba. Unknown to Muhammad they had resolved to let the first man who walked into the sanctuary decide the matter. Entering the holy place, Muhammad placed the Black Stone on a blanket and told each tribe to lift a corner. Then he personally laid the meteorite in its new niche. Muslims believe the Ka'ba is the spot where Abraham prepared to sacrifice his son Ishmael at God's command.

Muhammad spent six months in solitary meditation in a cave at the foot of Mount Hira and it was here that the Angel Gabriel appeared to him with the command to "Proclaim!," thrice-repeated. Ths vision's instructions were precise: "Proclaim in the name of the Lord, the creator who created man from a clot of blood. Proclaim! Your Lord is most gracious. It is he who has taught man by the pen that which he does not know."

It was the year AD 610 and Muhammad was forty. He began to preach the new faith of Islam, which was being gradually revealed to him as the Koran, through his sojourns in the desert. Some of this religion was already familiar to the Arabs who knew about the monotheistic teachings of the Jews and Christians.

Muhammad was expelled from Mecca because his new beliefs threatened the town's tolerant religious atmosphere, on which rested its commercial prosperity. In the year AD 622 he and a small group of followers traveled to a small town, now known as Medina, 200 miles northwest of Mecca. This migration became known as the Hegira (or Hidjra) and it marks the starting point of the Muhammadan era. In the remaining decade of his life the Prophet laid the foundation of Islam, a word which literally means submission—to the will of one God, Allah, the Compassionate, the Merciful.

In Medina Muhammad's apostleship found more general acceptance and this gave him not only more religious authority but its concomitant in Islam, political power. In theory, even when the Prophet was in a position to assert his authority, the inhabitants were not compelled to accept his teachings; his mission is described as one of preaching only. Yet many were soon persuaded to join his cause. The Jews who inhabited Medina and the surrounding country stood out stubbornly, mainly because, as they saw it, Muhammad was giving mutilated and confused versions of stories he had heard from them or from the Christians. The Jews claimed to have the original and authentic source of the stories. Muhammad retaliated by accusing them of falsifying the scriptures. When this had no effect he eliminated the danger they represented by slaughter or banishment. It is from this time that we can really date the Arab-Jew/Israeli conflict. If it was right for Muhammad of all people to kill Jews it became right for Muammar Gaddafi, Yasser Arafat and President Sadat.

When he had a strong enough force Muhammad marched against the unbelievers at Mecca, partly for vengeance, partly because it was essential for his prestige that he capture the traditional sanctuary of his own tribe —and capture it he did. He made Mecca the holy city of Muslims, destroyed all the idols and purified the Ka'ba so that it could become the most holy place of Allah. Other cities followed Medina as the capital of Muhammadanism but Mecca always remained the spiritual center of Islam.

Muhammad took the Arabian tribes by charisma, unifying them and calling on them to wage a "Holy War" in which those who died fighting the infidel would go to paradise. This conviction is still deeply rooted in Muslim

thinking. Before his death Muhammad had gathered under his banner most of the inhabitants of Arabia. The
exceptions were the Jews, Christians and Magians, who
were permitted to remain in their own faiths provided
they recognized Muhammad's political overlordship by
the payment of a poll-tax (jizya), a form of protection
money. But he excluded them and all "unbelievers" from
the communal life by forbidding them to enter Mecca—a
prohibition still in force.

While Muhammad was married to Khadijah he took no
other wife but he was married eleven times in all, mostly
to divorcees and widows. His sons died in infancy but
four daughters survived. The traditions show that Muhammad had a healthy male appreciation of women, and
that he was indeed a *gentle*man, giving comfort to women
when they came to him with problems.

Muhammad's own methods of rising to power were
emulated by many later Islamic rulers. These methods
need to be understood, for 1400 years later they still
sanctify certain attitudes and strategems. Muhammad
used religious power for his own political ends, and certainly he seems to have considered that the ends justified
the means. Militarily he was ruthless—at least once he
tolerated massacre. Politically he was an opportunist,
seeking alliances where he could find them. For a religious leader he was remarkably aggressive and impatient.
The most powerful factor of his life was his unshakable
belief that he had been called by Allah; this conviction
exercised an enormous influence on others of his time and
through them on posterity. The certainty with which he
announced Allah's words and commands was to prove
enduringly compelling.

Some of his more fanatical followers have tried to
falsify the life of Muhammad by introducing not only
major fictions but many trivialities. Also many Muslims
drew a picture of Muhammad that would not be inferior
to the Christian picture of Jesus. In their efforts to
achieve this Muhammad's admirers went contrary to his
intentions—they make him perform miracles such as are
related of Jesus.

The miracle related in St. John's Gospel (2:1–11) has

served as a pattern for a series of miraculous legends which were inserted at an early date into the biography of Muhammad. The Prophet was able to increase in a supernatural manner a supply of water and at another time the supply of food. The Muslim biographers of the Prophet try even more eagerly to emulate Christians in developing the miraculous feature of the healing of the sick by the Prophet; this took place, they say, through the efflux of a healing power which dwelt in his body or in things that belonged to him.

In retrospect we can see that when Muhammad died prematurely in 632 Islam was only a flickering light illuminating a small part of Arabia. He did not found a dynasty because he had no son, though his daughter Fatima had married his cousin, Ali, and had two sons. One was murdered in 669 and Hussin, the younger grandson, was a victim of the massacre at Karbála in 680. These tragic deaths caused the spiritual emotion which created the breakaway Shi'a Islam as a way of giving immortality to the Prophet's line.

Despite the lack of male heirs for Muhammad, the dim light of Islam became a flame. Just how it devoured the surrounding lands so quickly is still not fully explicable but one reason must be that there was no lapse in command after Muhammad's death. The office of the Caliphate came into being to provide a successor who had rank and dignity. The Caliphs had no spiritual role in the way that Muhammad had, but they were master administrators. The first was Abu Bakr, then 'Umar, both fathers-in-law of Muhammad. Three of the first four Caliphs were murdered, a token of the violence which was to permeate the Islamic world. But if Caliphs were expendable the Caliphate endured, surviving until 1924 when Kemal Ataturk abolished it.

Under the early Caliphs Islamic warriors rapidly conquered Syria, Mesopotamia (Iraq) and Egypt, and they founded Baghdad and Cairo. With tremendous impetus the Islamic fire engulfed faiths and cultures in all directions. In the centenary year of the Prophet's death the Islamic armies had pushed as far as Poitiers in France but were here beaten and turned back across the Pyrenees.

Despite this setback, within two centuries of Muhammad's death Islam dominated the great sweep of territory from southern Spain to northern India. The Muslims would remain dominant in Spain for another seven centuries.

To the east of its origins Islam gained a foothold in Sumatra and Java through Muslim traders in the thirteenth and fourteenth centuries. It spread, as much by peaceful colonization as military conquest in this region, throughout Java, to Sumatra and on to the Malay peninsula, then moving further east to the Moluccas, the Sulu Archipelago and parts of the Philippines, notably Mindanao.

The Islamic tide of conquest was so powerful that to Muslim historians it forced history upon the world. "History surrendered to our will," as one of my proud Saudi friends has told me. It probably seemed that way to his ancestors.

The Christian Crusaders, the élite of Europe, ventured to Arabia to fight the Muslims on their home ground and by their own declared value—those of religion. Their mission, as they saw it, was to recover the Holy Places of Christendom, a jihad against jihad. These valiant, vainglorious knights of many nationalities fought and died in eight principal crusades between 1095 and 1272 but in the end the relentless Muslim pressure was too much for them. From the East came Turkish, Mongol and Tartar invaders, drawn as always to fighting and conquest for their own sake. Virtually irresistible in their ferocity, they occupied Muslim domains—and then submitted to Islam, usually quite quickly. Either way, by outstaying their enemies, as they had the Crusaders, or by converting them, as with the barbarians, Islam won. The spirit of Muhammad was triumphant.

Great as these martial achievements were for the effect they had on the world they were even more important for the effect they had on Islam. They gave the faith and its followers a taste and an instinct for overlordship, a sublime confidence and an assurance so positive that it became habitual. Islam was achieving its destiny with a momentum and completeness that affected all Muslims emotionally and a great many intellectually. With so many other races and tribes of people under its rule, and with their beliefs subject to Islam, it was no wonder that Islamic leaders thought they held History itself at the point of the sword. Spiritually they were invulnerable because they wore the armor of jihad. In practice their sheer verve, energy and ferocity were almost unbeatable. Their astonishing conquests confirmed the character of Islam as strong, self-confident, omnipotent. From these characteristics came its unyielding, hostile attitude to everything that lay outside itself.

After it left Arabia—perhaps *because* it left Arabia—Islam took on a culture, much of it borrowed, of such refinement and such achievement that it has largely eradicated the memory of its accompanying cruelty. The new culture contributed much to art and knowledge of many kinds and produced here and there the type of paradise described in the Koran. The Alhambra of Granada, the palace of the last Muslim rulers in Spain, with its tree-like columns, ponds, fountains and gardens is probably the finest example of what the Muslims expected to find in the after life.

The great architectural triumphs of early Islam are still among the most impressive constructions in the world. The mausoleum of Timur the Lame (Tamarlane) at Samarkand is breathtaking and the Mosque of Omar in Jerusalem—the so-called Blue Mosque—is a delicate and durable testimony to craftsmen who must have loved what they created. The early Muslims built great hospitals and libraries, the most opulent being the palace in Shiraz, Persia, where the library had 360 rooms, each room a different shape and with its distinctive style and color scheme. The most famous of all Islamic monuments is the Taj Mahal, which a good many visitors believe is too beautiful to be described.

Sooner or later all imperialists are beaten by even stronger empire-builders, or they absorb so much of the cultures which they conquer that they lose their initial drive, and thus fall to marauders in an earlier stage of their cycle of rise-decline-fall. To the orthodox Muslim Arab—the non-Arabs are less affected—Islam's history came to an end in 1258 with the sack of Baghdad by the Mongols, in 1492 with the fall of Granada and the end of Muslim Spain, and in 1517 when the Turks conquered Egypt.

Islam went into a dark age where it would remain for more than four centuries. History had gone wrong.

4

"DISTRESS, MISFORTUNE AND WEAKNESS"

Its fervor spent, Islam remained in a state of frustrated impotence. Unable to push their frontiers further, the Muslim leaders were, in any case, constantly involved with internal conflicts and competing dynastic claims. In one way or another they had imposed their will on the non-Muslims in their midst, even when the non-Muslims were in the majority. Foreigners fought battles on Muslim land but usually not for that land. Napoleon had a brief flirtation with Egypt and explorers, mostly British, ventured into Islam's depths. Then came the imperial nineteenth century when states and people began to feel pressure from Western Europeans in more and more aspects of their life. The British, French and Dutch were empire-building and, almost before they were aware of it, the Muslims found that their lands were those empires.

The conquerors were mercantile and militaristic Christians who could not be absorbed and integrated, as the Turks, Tartars and Mongols had been. Moreover, they could rarely be defeated by force of arms, as hundreds of bloody encounters showed. The only Islamic people who posed any threat to the West were the Turks, but until the twentieth century the dangers from that quarter were indirect.

Western scholars, administrators, explorers and missionaries were busy analyzing and dissecting Islam with a thoroughness that was characteristically European. In 1883 Ernest Renan, the French philosopher and historian, in a famous lecture on Islam and science, claimed that they were incompatibles. "Anyone who has been in the East or in Africa will have been struck by the hidebound spirit of the true [Islamic] believer, by this kind of iron circle which surrounds his head, rendering him absolutely closed to science, incapable of learning anything or of opening himself to a new idea."

Lord Cromer, Viceroy of Egypt, thought that as a religion Islam was a "noble" monotheism but that as a social system it was a complete failure. "Islam keeps women in a position of inferiority ... crystalizes religion and law into an inseparable and immutable whole, with the result that all elasticity is taken out of the whole system ... it permits slavery ... its general tendency is towards intolerance of other faiths ... it does not encourage the development of logical thought ..."

For a long time Western writers described Islam as a "sensual" religion, chiefly because the Koran permits a man to take as many as four wives. It was against this kind of misunderstanding that Richard Burton, the great nineteenth-century traveler and Orientalist who knew Arab Muslim life intimately, protested "... Can we call that faith sensual which forbids a man to look upon a statue or a picture? Which condemns even the most moderate use of inebrients, and indeed is not certain upon the subject of coffee and tobacco? Which will not allow even the most harmless game of chance or skill? Which vigorously prohibits music, dancing, and even poetry and works of fiction upon any but strictly religious subjects? Above all things, which debars man from the charms of female society, making sinful a glance at a strange woman's unveiled face? A religion whose votaries must pray five times a day at all seasons ... Whose yearly fast often becomes one of the severest trials to which the human frame can be exposed? To whom distant pilgrimage with all its trials and hardships is obligatory at least once in life?"*

*The Jew, the Gipsy and El Islam.

It is doubtful if the Muslim politicians, patriots and scholars—there were few of these—read what the foreigners were saying about them, but they were certainly conscious of Islam's decline. In 1880–81 the now highly respected Jamal al-Din al-Afghani was writing that "distress, misfortune and weakness besiege all classes of Muslims from every side." Every Muslim, he said, was keeping his eyes and ears open for signs of the sage and renewer who would appear to reform the minds and souls of Muslims, eradicate their corruption and re-educate them.

A few pretenders appeared, proclaimed jihad and fought bloody wars but their successes, such as they were, took place in the desert and hardly disturbed the occupying imperialists. By the beginning of the twentieth century most Muslim states had lost their sovereignty to some form of foreign imperial control, and those that maintained independence did so in fear and apprehension. This situation presented Muslim thinkers and leaders with great intellectual and emotional difficulties. Islam demands of its believers that they accept that God ruled the world and that the Divine Will initiated and controlled political change, as well as all other changes among men. So why should Allah abandon the true believers and favor Christians? Christians were infidels—they had compounded their original religious errors with a failure to recognize the mission of Muhammad. For a great many Muslims it was logical to suppose that Allah was punishing Islam for failing to conform to His laws as revealed to Muhammad.

The remedy was equally logical—reform by reversion to the original precepts, purification by eradication of corruption. The Wahhabis of Arabia, the followers of the Mahdi (the "Expected One") in the Sudan, and a good many other less notable Islamic spokesmen wholly accepted this cure and applied it rigorously, to the point of jihad.

At the beginning of the twentieth century the Muhammadan world was seen as an alien force which Christendom had every reason to fear. In retrospect this fear seems irrational but at this time the Ottoman (Turkish)

Empire was great and powerful, so the military threat was in being. The collapse of the Ottomans and their retreat from the Arab lands at the end of World War I opened the way for Western, principally British, physical dominance over the Middle East. Soon after this the Arab élites embraced the Western faith in science and technology and hungrily accepted many of the West's social and cultural attitudes. This all led most Western statesmen to believe that the Muslim faith was declining as a political power; unlike Renan and Cromer, they were too ignorant to understand that Islam is politics, religion, economy, and culture all in one.

Britain, in recruiting Arabs to fight against the Turks—who happened to be their coreligionists—inadvertently rekindled the flame of Islam. Those victories of 1916–18 in the Arabian deserts—though militarily of a very minor nature—reminded the Muslims of Arabia of what it must have been like in the great days of Islamic conquest.

But in the earlier decades of the twentieth century many Muslims could accept neither the extreme notion that they were guilty of terrible disobedience nor the other extremity of rigorous reform. They saw Islam as some tremendous historical error or aberration which had to be done away with. The most famous of the rejectionists was Mustapha Kemal (Ataturk) who "abolished" the Islamic inheritance, while keeping "Muhammadanism" as a religion. He swept away all the trappings of Islam, the priestly vestments, the stultifying influence of submission to Koranic law, even the fez—which Kemal saw as "a sign of ignorance, fanaticism, of hatred to civilization and progress."

In a speech to parliament Kemal said: "Could a civilized nation tolerate a mass of people who let themselves be led by the nose by a herd of Sheikhs, Dedes, Seids, Tschelebis, Babas and Emirs [types of Islamic holy men]; who entrusted their destiny and their lives to chiromancers, magicians, dice-throwers and amulet sellers? Ought one to conserve in the Turkish State, in the Turkish Republic, elements and institutions such as those which had for centuries given the nation the appearance of being other than it really was? Would one not therewith have committed the greatest, most irreparable error to the cause of progress and reawakening? [We wished] to prove that our people think neither in a fanatical nor a reactionary manner ... to destroy the spirit of [Islamic] despotism for ever."

Though the British and French Western influence was profound in all the Middle and Near East Muslim world, in India British values prevailed alone and in Indonesia the Dutch implanted Western values. In the 1920s an Egyptian schoolteacher, Hassan al-Banna, wrote that Western values and culture were "the silken curtain which conceals the hands of greed and dreams of exploitation."

Al-Banna founded the Society of Muslim Brethren (better known in the West as the Muslim Brotherhood) which was to become the most powerful Islamic organization since the heyday of the Wahhabi movement, on whose ideas the Muslim Brotherhood is based. The Wahhabi community was founded by 'Abd al-Wahhib (1703–1787), whose doctrines are regarded as extreme even in his homeland of Saudi Arabia. His principal argument is that all objects of worship other than Allah are false and all who worship them deserve death; it is apostasy to introduce the name of a prophet, saint or angel into a prayer.

No less extreme, al-Banna became known as Murshid al-'amm (the Supreme Guide) and spread his secret organization throughout Egypt, Sudan, Syria, Lebanon, Jordan, Palestine and North Africa. His principal demand was a return to orthodox Islam, doing away with all innovations since the third century of Islam, along Wahhabi lines.

During World War II neither the Brotherhood nor any other movement made much headway, since most of the Muslim world was a battlefield for the warring great powers. Soon after World War II the Western imperialist nations began, most reluctantly, to withdraw from their Islamic and other colonies. And a great paradoxical irony occurred—the West brought itself into disrepute among the Muslims, and especially the Arabs, by doing those very things which the Arabs had been demanding. It removed itself from the Near East and Middle East, a withdrawal culminating in Britain's ignominious abandonment of the Persian Gulf and Aden. The British, brought up on a diet of Christian humility, might have seen this as enlightened, as a recognition that the days of empire were over. The Arabs, raised on the headier Islamic diet of pride, saw the British as weak and decadent and in consequence humiliated. They no longer had any respect for Britain.

For many centuries the Muslims had been objects in world politics, minor actors in a drama whose marginal position on the stage was determined by others—and in the others' interest. After World War II they found themselves occupying the center of the stage from time to time, and doing so on their own terms, as chief heroes or chief villains.

To take the analogy further, as they have become more conscious of the importance of their role, they challenge the audience to pay attention to them, sometimes rather in the way an actor conscious of his power might march to the front of the stage and say to his audience, "If you don't pay attention to me I'll stop the show!"

During this rapid process from crowd player to star (and here we had better end the metaphor) the Muslims, especially the Arab Muslims, found they had allies—the enemies of those who had controlled them for so long. Most notably, the Russians moved in as the British moved out. Other allies appeared from among other peoples who also sought to express their own identity—the Third World nations. The support of these nations increased as the Muslims' power and wealth increased. This was no coincidence but dictated by political expediency.

For a time—perhaps until the mid-1960s—the Muslim states were flattered by the attention paid to them by the wealthy industrial powers of West and East. The capitals of Islam were full of business representatives from Britain, America, France, Germany, Poland, U.S.S.R., Czechoslovakia, Japan and many other countries. The realization that these nations needed the Muslims more than the Muslims needed them produced heady delights in institutions as disparate as the halls of al Ahzar and the palaces of Riyadh. A few dreamers—the Shah of Iran was one—went on dreaming; he was still flattered by American courtship and the privilege the U.S.A. accorded him by extending to him the exclusive right to buy certain sophisticated weaponry.

One day the Muslim Arabs realized with shock and delight that there were twenty-two Arab states. This led to another quick count to discover that they were part of forty-four Muslim states, a sizeable political bloc, one to challenge any other bloc such as "the West" or the Communist bloc, or any permutation of powers.

This bloc was not apparent in the unifying sense of the Western democratic powers or the Eastern communist countries. Within the Islamic countries there was, as always, fierce competition for power, great violence and much bloodshed, with many plots, coups, assassinations and executions. Brutal conflicts took place between tribes, sects, nations and ideologies. Muslim decapitated, disemboweled and mutilated Muslim throughout the Islamic world. Torture was commonplace as rulers clung desperately to power.

The Arab Muslims were more or less united on only one subject—the desire to expel Israel from the Islamic world. Too little attention has been given to the religious nature of the Arabs' ceaseless hostility against Israel. The Arabs protest about Israeli seizure of Arab land, about Israel's being merely an outpost of the U.S., about Israeli "expansionism"—but this is sophistry. Their main objection to Israel is one they try not to speak about too openly, except among themselves, because they know the West is touchy about religious prejudice. To Muslims the issue is clear: Israel is inhabited by Jews and Islam proclaims that Jews and Christians are its enemies. As the Muslims see it, Christians put Israel where it is so they are as blameworthy as the Jews themselves. The members of both religions are as infidel now as they were at the time of the Crusades.

If one is to fight against those who do not "believe" it becomes necessary—in order to denounce them and threaten them with punishment—to attribute to them much responsibility for their unbelief. The Muslims are constantly attributing responsibility to the Israelis. In the history of Islam practically all the political wars, even among Muslims, were defined in religious terms with the religious leadership taking an active part in expounding the issues at stake.

The Israeli victories in the wars of 1948, 1956 and 1967 were not, to the Muslims, so much military as religious defeats. Islam was supposed always to triumph, but defeat at the hands of the great Western Christian powers could be rationalized on the grounds that they had numerically great and powerful armies, centuries ahead of the rest of the world in military technology. Subjugation by Western arms was a disgrace but no great shame was involved. But defeat by a handful of Jews was a stain of shame on Islam.

No wonder, then, that the Muslims were ready to fight their battles against Israel on a "carpet of blood," when they launched the October 1973 war. Military historians generally agree that Israel had the upper hand when a ceasefire ended the October War, twenty-two days after it began. Nevertheless, the initial Arab successes were hailed by Muslim commentators as the greatest victories since Saladin defeated the Crusaders at the Battle of Hittin in 1187 and recaptured Jerusalem. Muslims all over the world took pride in the war's early Egyptian-Syrian triumphs. When the Americans prevented the Israeli army from destroying the Egyptian Third Army, which the Israelis had surrounded and cut off, they were laying the foundation not only for the myth of Arab near-victory in the Yom Kippur War but for the resurgence of Islam.

The Muslims did not understand their full power potential. Their Arab oil-producing group tried, rather tentatively at first, to blackmail the West by the threat of oil sanctions. To their delight, the threat frightened the West and the subsequent cut in oil supplies brought the "great powers" to heel. A Muslim who was then an academic and is now a diplomat in a sensitive area (and hence reluctantly I agree to his request not to be identified) told me at the time: "It was the most satisfying time for Muslims in hundreds of years. The Christian West, not to mention the pagan Japanese and Indians and others, were whimpering in fear. Having been the bullies' victims for a long time we were now the bullies! The students at my university were saying, 'Now we'll rub the Christians' noses in the shit!' "

Whether under republics, military republics or monarchies (there are no Western-type democracies in the Muslim world) the Muslims now display several attitudes the world has come to recognize. One is their willingness to make alliances of one sort or another purely on the basis of expediency, such as Egypt's deals with the Soviets. Another is their scorn of Western—or of Christian—pleas for moderation in the matter of punishments (amputation, flogging, execution), of oil prices, and of attitudes to Israel. Most importantly, Muslim leaders have learned how to make demands—for money, armaments. These take many forms. Syria and Iraq demanded arms from the Soviets as the price for adopting an anti-U.S. stance; Saudi Arabia demanded U.S. weapons systems as the price for remaining "moderate" on oil prices and in relation to Israel; Algeria demanded money from France as the price of remaining pro-French.

Political extremism comes easily to much of the Islamic world for three reasons—low standard of living and education (despite oil wealth), the absence of democracy, profound resentment against the West. The standard of living has been rising for some Muslims but the generally low level enables Arab Muslim leaders to pursue political goals without regard for the economic consequences—an agricultural society, such as Syria, is hardly aware that changes in the slight superstructure of industry and commerce can affect its own welfare also.

The low level of education is conducive to political extremism in two ways. First, it takes hyperbole and constant repetition to arouse the masses. But the monotony and hopelessness of their existence makes them responsive to ideological appeals and exhortations from a determined pedagogue. Khomeini has illustrated this in Iran; he worked on the ignorance and repressed hostility of the mobs to bring them to violence—with the help of student agitators organized by the mullahs.

As the Muslim countries develop their urban working classes so they will have large groups susceptible to manipulation. Inexperienced in politics and industry, often recent country dwellers who have come to the cities for a better life, the urban workers are easily swayed by promises, especially those made in the name of Islam or by religious leaders.

A more volatile and important group are the students of secondary schools and universities. Articulate, politically conscious and ambitious, these young people are also politically unstable, the result of frustration and exasperation. They rarely find jobs commensurate with their intelligence and training. It is easy for any experienced agitator to bring them into the streets to protest about almost anything. The core of most city demonstrations, they are more militantly Islamic now than ever before. Governments, which sometimes use the students for their own ends—to demonstrate against the West for instance—then find them difficult to control when they demonstrate against their own government.

The absence of democratic processes in Muslim states encourages extremism since there is no orderly, legitimate way in which to show dissent. When disputes over doctrine and fundamental policy are not allowed expression they become heightened and self-perpetuating by this repression. A second danger is that lack of democratic checks on the rulers, which we take for granted in the West, enables Muslim leaders to ignore public opinion for so long that the situation can become explosive, as it did in Iran before the revolution.

5

"NO COMPASSION FOR WEAKNESS"

Having seen Islam in its days of glory and then in its period of decline and "shame" before again finding the road to its destiny, it is necessary to look at Islamic society and the Muslim mind.

That there *is* a Muslim mind was noted by Arnold Toynbee who, like others before him, observed that the Muslim is indifferent to anything that does not directly concern his life in this world or the next. "This is not simply theological," Toynbee wrote,* "It is the very texture of the Muslim mind. We can say: 'This is an interesting book'; in Arabic you cannot express this idea... Even curiosity, in the highest and finest sense, we cannot render [in Arabic]... The free, self-determining, self-developing soul may not walk its own path, however innocently, but must fit itself to the scheme and pattern..."

The idea of an "interesting" book or the concept of curiosity cannot be expressed because Muslims who have not had the benefits of a Western education live in an intellectual straitjacket from which the ability to make abstract judgments of a book has yet to struggle free.

While Toynbee and many other Westerners identify a

*A Study of History, 1954.

28

Muslim mind, a few social anthropologists claim that there is no such thing as "Islamic society." Some societies are partly molded by Islam, they say, but they are also formed by their position in the physical world, their inherited language and culture, their economic possibilities and the accidents of their political history. This academic hypothesis, supported by pure academicians such as Albert Hourani, ignores the simple fact that many states of Muslim peoples *consider themselves* as "Islamic societies." It is this self-label, this claim to be distinguished as Islamic, which produces such a thing as "Islamic society." The important fact in the late twentieth century is that Islam will be what Muslims say it is.

A great many prominent Muslims implicitly contest in their writings Professor Hourani's observation. Hassan al-Banna, the founder of the Muslim Brotherhood, wrote that "Any innovation not based on religion is a departure from rectitude which must be resisted and eliminated by every means." Only in an Islamic society would such a statement make any sense. Inamullah Khan, leader of the World Muslim Congress, announced, "Islam does not need to be modernized. Islam has always been modern."* Only in an Islamic society could such a claim be taken seriously.

Islam claims authority over everything the Muslim does, including his political and economic activities. For the devout Muslim a reference to a "secular Muslim country" is meaningless, a contradiction in terms; according to the Koran a Muslim country is Islamic and to apply the adjective "secular" to it is pointless and even insulting.

It is difficult for the West, where religion plays such a small part, or no part at all, in the lives of the vast majority, to understand the extent to which Islam is a whole way of life, reinforced daily by frequent communal observance. With such uniformity of direction it is surprising that so many divisions survive in the Muslim world. Perhaps this is because the intoxication of national

*In an essay in *God and Man in Contemporary Islamic Thought*, ed. Charles Malik, Beirut, 1972.

liberation has anesthetized Muslims against all the forms of subjection that survive; though powerful, they are so subtle and insidious that they are often almost unnoticed. Some Muslims *have* noticed. I am especially impressed with the writings of Mr. Muhammad Fadhel Jamali, a devoutly Islamic Iraqi, who was arrested when General Kassem came to power in Iraq in 1958. For no good reason Mr. Jamali was condemned to death but reprieved; his new sentence was commuted to fifty-five years in prison and a fine of £100,000. He was released after eighteen months, a period he spent in writing letters of moral and spiritual instruction to his son. In one letter he wrote:

> He who studies carefully the struggle between various religious groups in the Arab world is struck with bewilderment by what he sees in terms of selfishness, arrogance, pedantry, perversion of truth and lack of humility before it, and loss of the spirit of unity, brotherhood, love and mercy which emanates from the religion of Islam.*

In other letters, Mr. Jamali wrote:

> The stagnation and backwardness in the Muslim World today are due to the failure to uphold the teachings of the holy religion which urges action, construction and brotherhood.
> Islamic society today is mainly backward and stagnant. This is due to ignorance, to fanaticism which kills the freedom of thought, to selfishness ...
> The conflicts among the Muslims and the destructive wars from within and without in the past and the quarrels between the rulers have led to what we see today in terms of ignorance, fanaticism, poverty and disease among Muslims.

A good Iraqi, Mr. Jamali is not criticizing Islam but the inability of Muslims to live up to the precepts of

*Letters on Islam, Oxford University Press, 1965.

Islam. The greatest failure in Islamic social and political life, he says, has been the failure of Muslims to practice "genuine democratic life." His concept of "democracy" has no connection with the Western definition; by democracy he means morality, which in turn depends on the "religious spirit."

Despite his plea for an end to fanaticism, like my orthodox Muslim Mr. Jamali would argue that Moslem countries should be one-party states. By Islamic standards, this is logical. If there is a righteous party it follows, in Islamic thought, that other parties must be unrighteous and therefore have no right to exist. The concept of there perhaps being more than one righteous party is incomprehensible. For this reason, it is a gross error to believe that any Middle Eastern Muslim country is governed in a benign way. It is simply that some, like Tunisia, are less despotic than others, such as Saudi Arabia. The ruling Saud family holds all power and wields it with an intensity made possible by the backing of the religious leaders. There is no legal opposition, no trades union organization, no constitution, no elections.

No wonder that Professor Hourani can refer to "the fragile human achievements of the Muslims."

The greatest human achievement in a century, I believe, was that of President Sadat in reaching a peace treaty with Israel. Even if, in the end, his opponents destroy the treaty, President Sadat has set a tremendous example—he has thrown off the restrictions of Islam and acted out of humanitarian concern for his own people.

More generally, Islam is a coercive force which compels the people to be subservient to the state. Saudi Arabia is an extreme example; here the religious police—the mutawwas—have terrorized the population and enforced the seclusion of women and the observance of prayer. Political prisoners are forced to read the Koran aloud for hours each day. Islam has permeated the society of all the Near and Middle East and of Pakistan so thoroughly that all political and social conflict takes a religious form to a degree not found in other societies.

This permeating thread of religiosity has been noticed

bv Western editorial writers. Typical is a comment from
The Guardian Weekly:*

> There has not been a time in recent experience
> when across the swathe of non-Arab Muslim coun-
> tries from Afghanistan to Turkey, taking in Pakistan
> and Iran along the way, so much purely political
> discontent was surfacing violently and at the same
> time expressing itself in religious euphemisms with
> which the West is only half familiar.

The West is not even half familiar with a particular
characteristic of Islamic thought designed to end all in-
quiry—the words "God knows." This answer is adequate
for any situation, a neat way of avoiding an answer,
evading a decision, saving face and getting out of difficulties.

In his time President Nasser avoided difficulties by his
approach to problem solving: With a deeper knowledge
of Islamic peoples than many of his contemporaries, he
used religion as a means rather than as an end. He once
pointed out that exhortations to win a football match for
all sorts of stated moral or religious reasons could take
the place of the necessary training for the game. I do not
believe that he was advocating exhortations wholly in
place of training, but he knew that any leader of Muslims,
by giving them religious or moral cause or reason, could
induce them to grow more rice, have more (or fewer)
chi'dren, fight more valiantly in battle.

In any case it would be difficult to give Muslims adequate "training for the game." Almost 70 per cent of
them are rural dwellers, farmers and fishermen in the
familiar occupational patterns of any under-developed
country. Their hopes of a better life are frustrated by
illiteracy, lack of technology, rejection of innovation—
indeed almost aggressive unwillingness to expose them-
se'ves to it. Because of centuries of isolation they are
unable to develop progressive social institutions, such as

*London, January 7, 1979.

co-operative farming methods and children's right to education.

Nevertheless, even the rural illiterate share something of Islam's new assertiveness. Given extra impetus by frustration, this assertiveness can be seen in identification with Islam and the glories can be restored, in seeking to reestablish the laws of the past, in hounding scapegoats within Islam and abroad considered responsible for Islam's continued corruption and difficulties. The chief scapegoats are the Jews of Israel since they are conveniently close, and it is so easy to blame the establishment of the State of Israel for the great problems within Arab countries.

Apologists for Islam prefer to assess the assertiveness and exercise of power as defensive, though Geoffrey Godsell of the *Christian Science Monitor* charitably sees Islam's assertiveness as "the plangent and defiant cry of the adherents of a great religion which has yet to come to terms theologically and convincingly with today's world."

The distinction between militant Islam and Muslim nationalism is confused. Some Western students of Islam insist that there is no connection and that in some ways militant Islam is not even pan-Islam. They base this assertion on the policies of the Muslim Brotherhood, the Jamaat-i-Islami Party in Pakistan and the Masjumi Party in Indonesia; all three have renounced and denounced nationalistic and pan-Islamic ideas. The leaders of these three powerful parties see nationalism as a foe of Islam because it has a purely political approach and is therefore, in fundamentalist Islamic thought, a heresy. When you suggest to these particular Muslims that in fighting the Western nations who controlled so much of the Muslim world they were nevertheless engaging in a political act, they will tell you that this was only a means to an end. All Muslims were fighting to eject the "Christian and imperialistic West," but those Muslims who then wanted a modern type nation were false to Islam. The Western scholars who deny the existence of pan-Islamism say that such a movement could have no force because it is essentially secular and political and therefore must be in conflict with the Islamic zealots. This reasoning will not stand up to the counter-argument that it is the zealots themselves who are creating the pan-Islamic movement by calling for—and where possible enforcing—a return to the Shari'a (Islamic law).

Militant national Islam or pan-Islam, neither will tolerate the "modern approach" urged on them by some Muslim scholars resident outside the Islamic world. Most religions accept that there are many people with reasoning minds and the hierarchy then elaborates the doctrines to make them acceptable to philosophical thought—or at least to rational thought. Islam singularly fails to do this—though "fails" is my Western value-judgment word. No Muslim considers it necessary to make Islamic doctrines "acceptable," so failure is an irrelevance.

Islamic leaders have always looked suspiciously at philosophy, at any "searching for the truth"—Toynbee's "highest curiosity"—because it comes perilously close to blasphemy. In any case, philosophy is secular and has no place in Islam. We of the West can rationally set out to trace the sources and developments of the ideas expounded in the Koran but such an activity is meaningless to the Muslim—and blasphemous, since the Koran is literally the word of God. In traditionalist Islam improvement is not possible, because the examples to be followed belong to the ever more remote past. Muhammad's early followers were the best generation; their successors, the second best. From then on, the world has been deteriorating and will continue to deteriorate until it comes to its appointed end. The living generation is not permitted to change the inherited ways—for change can only be for the worse.

J. Stewart-Robinson, formerly of the University of Michigan, a specialist in the role of tradition in Islamic society, says:*

> Innovation in religious matters (and religion covers everything relevant to the good life) is to be rejected, the innovator liable to punishment. The

*The Traditional Near East, Prentice-Hall, 1966.

reformer therefore either adduces prophetic or koranic witness for his proposal or advocates the return to the golden age of primitive Islam. The pattern may not be abandoned or even modified; it may only be stripped of accretions and freed of distortions that have accumulated in the course of time. The heroic, the creative, age is past . . .

Such a rigidity of mind means that Islam is artificially protected from criticism, which does the faith a great disservice. If debate were possible Muslims might well be able to express points of view and advance deductions which have escaped foreign students. It is almost impossible to publish in Arabic or Persian, or in most of the languages of the Islamic world, any critical study of Islam, whether scientific or popular, no matter how knowledgeable and sympathetic the writer might be. Under Islam everything is Divine Plan. This may help partly to explain one of the most striking aspects of the Muslims, especially among the Arabic Muslims—the absence of doubt and inner guilt. There was a time when they felt no anxiety either but they do now and efforts to get rid of it are leading Muslims into ever more strident denunciations of the West, the Christians, Jews and Communists.

For the tradition-bound Muslim, there is even something sinful in engaging in long-range planning because it seems to imply that one does not put one's trust in divine providence. A century ago Ernest Renan denounced the "stupefying consequences of the brutal domination of Muslim dogma."*

Much more recently another French Islamophile, Alfred Guillaume, has explained that "An Islamic reformer, whether in secular or religious matters—and there is no clear line between them—has to reckon with the enormous power of tradition and the dead weight of inertia."†

A few courageous reformers have appeared from time to time. One was Sir Sayyid Ahmad Khan (1817–98) who wanted to restate and justify Islam in terms of modern thought. At Aligurgh, India, in 1875 he founded

*L'Islamisme et la science, Paris, 1883.
†Islam, Penguin, 1978 edition.

a college where religious education was combined with scientific studies. This first modernist organization in Islam was ferociously attacked and Sir Sayyid was denounced for "treason," "blasphemy" and every other crime against Allah. His movement prospered for a time but the college, now the Muslim University of Aligurgh, deteriorated into yet another fortress of fundamentalism.

Another even more liberal thinker, Sayyid Amir Ali, wrote that the Koran was the work of Muhammad (rather than the revealed word of God) though he stressed that this did not detract from its divinely inspired nature. Amir Ali was lucky not to have been assassinated.

Muslims consider themselves superior and over and over again their religious and nationalist leaders have told them that they must not submit to other peoples who are not as good as they are. These others may have had no intention of claiming to be better than Muslims, but Muslims are quick to take offense. "Adversaries of Allah" are all around, waiting to take advantage of them.

For this reason it is easy enough to instill in the Muslim mind a fear and distrust of foreigners and even a hatred of fellow Muslims, for as Muhammad Jamali from his Baghdad jail sadly explained to his son: "The majority of Muslims are ignorant and they sometimes fall easy victims to misleading, erroneous propaganda."

They are victims in another way, described by Dr. Sania Hamady, formerly of Miami University. A psychologist and sociologist and Lebanese Arab herself, Dr. Hamady says, "Islamic society is ruthless, stern and pitiless. It worships strength and has no compassion for weakness. Judgment is severe. It is rarely that a bad deed is forgiven . . ."*

Ayatollah Khomeini in Iran and General Zia in Pakistan are the latest in a long line of conquering zealots who have demonstrated the truth of Dr. Hamady's comments.

---

*Temperament and Character of the Arabs, Twayne, New York, 1960.

6

"MAKE WAR ON UNBELIEVERS"

Muhammad's system is rigid, positive and emphatic, says Professor H. A. R. Gibb, the greatest international authority on Islam.* Islam possesses these characteristics because of the Koran, the Hadith, the Sunna and the Shari'a (see Glossary). It is fundamental that without a knowledge of the Koran it is not possible to understand Islam and its adherents. Arab Muslims say that the Holy Book is untranslatable, furthermore, as the Koran was "sent down" to Muhammad in Arabic nobody is obliged on any holy grounds, such as obedience and submission, to translate it into other languages.

The Koran, Islam's one "miracle," is written in 114 suras or chapters, and in all is about the length of the Christian New Testament. It is uncertain whether the whole text was committed to writing during the Prophet's lifetime. Tradition relates that a few years after his death the scattered fragments were collected together from "scraps of parchment and leather, tablets of stone, ribs of palm branches, camels' shoulderblades, pieces of board and the breasts of men." The last phrase refers to the retentive memories of the Prophet's immediate followers.

*In his definitive work, *Islam: A Historical Survey*, Oxford University Press, 1969.

During the reign of the third Caliph, 'Uthman (644–56) the definitive Koran was established by a panel of theologian editors directed by Muhammad's "literary assistant" Zaid ibn Thabit. The arrangement of the Koran today is largely as it was authorized by 'Uthman.

The Koran is the final and unchangeable revelation of the divine will, abrogating all previous records of revelation, such as the Old and New Testaments. The Koran speaks of the years before Allah's message to Muhammad as years of "ignorance"—an implication that Christianity, Zoroastrianism and Judaism were of no consequence. The use of the word "ignorance" must be considered pejorative since the three established religions were well known, and it is significant that even Judaism, which had been in diaspora since the Roman destruction of the Temple in AD 70, had large numbers of native Arab adherents.

In public recitation the Koran is intoned or chanted in slow melodic phrases, the correct art of which is taught in Muslim seminaries. Whether you call this chanting "reading" or "singing" the vocal sounds of the human voice are at the root of Islamic music and for Sufi and Dervish they are the way into the trance state.

In Islamic life the ideal is to know the entire Koran by heart and many people do so know it. In various parts of the Muslim world I have had boys of ten and twelve pointed out to me as being able to recite the Koran right through. The Koran remains Arab children's universal reader, their grammar textbook. For the millions who do not read—and in most Muslim countries less than 50 per cent can—the Koran becomes oral history and moral guide.

All the Constitutions of the Arab countries are inspired by the Koran. In 1973 the Syrian regime wished to move away from this restriction. The result was riots in the mosques and a revolt that was harshly suppressed. Nevertheless, Damascus gave way to the ulama (religious leaders). Islam was declared the religion of the Head of State and the Koran was registered as one of the sources of national law. In contrast, the article of law defining the status of Christian minorities "disappeared" from the new system.

The pattern of submitting the civil law to the precepts of the Koran remains constant. In 1975 Hussein Kuwatli, a close collaborator of the Mufti of Beirut, published this pronouncement: "The Muslim cannot remain neutral in regard to the state. He is confronted with an alternative: Either the ruler and the government are Muslim in which case he is satisfied and supports them; or they are not Muslim, in which case he must reject them, oppose them and do everything in his power to change them, peacefully or by force, by openly declared or by secret activity . . . This is neither fanaticism nor prejudice. The question is much simpler. That is what Islam is all about . . . This religion was revealed thus—as a religion and as the state. It imposes itself upon individuals and groups, *for it is the law of God,* and it is impossible for us to substitute it with another." [My italics]

Nevertheless, some Muslims believe that Muhammad was the author of the Koran—that is, that he created it without divine help—and will openly say so in conversation. As Alfred Guillaume points out, there is no historical reason why they should not do so because the doctrine that the Koran is literally the word of God was not finally established until the third Islamic century. Guillaume always insisted that the Koran is nearer to Christianity than the system of Islam as it has developed down the centuries.

Guillaume's views are important because of his standing within the Muslim world. One-time visiting Professor of Arabic at Princeton and at the American University of Beirut, he was an elected Fellow of the Arab Academy at Damascus and of the Royal Academy of Baghdad. The University of Stambul chose him as its first foreign lecturer on Christian and Islamic theology.

Earlier scholars than Guillaume postulated a Jewish source with Christian additions, on the grounds that Jewish and Christian religious ideas were carried from Yemen to Mecca as a natural part of the cargo of the frequent caravans. More recently, as Professor Gibb has stated,

"Research has conclusively proved that the main external influences, including the Old Testament materials, can be traced back to Syriac Christianity."* The Muslim holy book certainly has links with both Christianity and Judaism, though the commandments of the Koran, unlike those of the Bible, often have an escape clause, as with "Do not kill any man, a deed God forbids, *except for rightful cause.*" [My italics.] It is this clause which justifies the fanatical reformer, such as Khomeini and Zia, in executing his rivals. They can easily produce a "rightful cause."

The Koran speaks for itself and it is enough to quote from it without interpretation. The quotations are selected to show how certain Koranic injunctions have affected Muslims' attitudes in modern times.

> *Do not pursue things you have no knowledge of.*
>
> (The Table, Sura 5)

This injunction has the effect of stifling curiosity. Even today most inhabitants of the Arab East know little, if anything, about the beliefs of those outside their community other than what has been told them by their fellow group members.

> *Do not falter or sue for peace; you will be the upper ones.*
>
> (Muhammad, Sura 47, 35)

This verse was quoted in the Great Mosque in Mecca just after the June 1967 war with Israel.

> *Men are in charge of women because Allah made the one of them to excel the other and because they spend of their property (to support women). So good women are obedient, guarding in secret [their*

---

*"The Koran is not the verbal manifestation of a Supreme Being dictating principles to be applied in every possible form of society but the work of a man inspired by certain ideals characteristic of the age in which he lived." Maxime Rodinson, *Islam and Capitalism*, Penguin, 1977.

private parts] that which Allah hath guarded. As for those from whom you fear rebellion, admonish them and banish them to beds apart, and beat them. Then if they obey you, seek not a way against them. Allah is ever High Exalted, Great.

(Women, Sura 4, 34)

Slay the polytheists wherever you find them.

(Repentance, Sura 9, 5)

This statement is said to have canceled no fewer than 124 verses which enjoined toleration and patience.

Surely Allah has bought from the believers their lives and their wealth. For theirs (in return) is the Garden (of Paradise). They shall fight in the way of Allah and shall slay and be slain; it is a promise which is binding.

(Repentence, 9:112)

The punishment of those who wage war against Allah and His apostle and strive to make mischief in the land is this, that they should be killed or crucified or their hands and feet should be cut off on opposite sides or they should be exiled from the land.

(The Table Spread 5:36)

They do blaspheme who say, "Allah is the Messiah, the son of Mary." . . . They are unbelievers who say "Allah is one of three." [The Christian belief in the Trinity]. They will be sternly punished.

(The Table, Sura 5)

Make war upon those who believe not . . . even if they be People of the Book [that is, Christians and Jews] until they have willingly agreed to pay the Jizya (tax) in recognition of their submissive state.

(Repentance, Sura 9, 29)

Islamic theologians quote this verse to support continued war against Israel.

Allah desires ease for you and He does not desire for you difficulty.

(The Cow, 11, 185)

You are the noblest nation that has ever been raised up for mankind.

(The Imrans, Sura 111)

The day will surely come when the unbelievers will wish that they were Muslims.

(El-Hijr, Sura 15)

These sayings, among others, are interpreted to mean that Muslims are the chosen people.

If they [the People of the Book—Christians and Jews] harm you, they can cause you no serious harm: and if they fight against you they will turn their backs and run away . . .

(The Imrans, Sura 111)

When the Christians who colonized the Islamic lands did not turn their backs and run, devout Muslims could only assume that this was Allah's way of showing his displeasure with Islam.

Believers, take neither Jews nor Christians for your friends. They are friends with one another. Whoever of you seeks their friendship shall become one of their number. Allah does not guide the wrongdoers . . . You see the faint-hearted hastening to woo them . . . Believers, do not seek the friendship of infidels and those who were given the Book before you . . . [that is, the Old and New Testaments].

(The Table, Sura 5)

Believers, do not make friends with any men other than your own people. They will spare no pains to corrupt you. They desire nothing but your ruin.

Their hatred is clear from what they say, but more violent is the hatred which their breasts conceal.

(The Imrans, Sura 111)

These verses were quoted against President Sadat for signing the Peace Treaty with Israel, and for cooperating with President Carter. Such passages make it virtually impossible for most Muslims to trust non-Muslims in commerce, politics or social life.

In several suras the paradise waiting for believers—and the hell for unbelievers—is vividly described. A comprehension of the joys of this paradise is necessary for anybody wishing to understand how Islam inspires its followers. No other religion can offer anything quite like it. As described in *That Which is Coming*, Sura 56, paradise is a delightful garden, the Abode of Peace, the abiding mansion, where the worthy dwell forever by flowing rivers, praising Allah, reclining on silken, jeweled lounges, enjoying heavenly food and drink in the company of dark-eyed maidens of perfect chastity and purity. Virtuous men "recline on couches raised on high in the shade of thornless sidrahs and clusters of banana palms, amid gushing waters and abundant fruits, unforbidden, never-ending."

This most perfect of places is only for those who have fought for Allah, those who have suffered for Him, and are godfearing, humble and charitable and forgiving.

The unworthy and the infidels are promised fire where they will forever abide without relief; even when they want a drink they will get only boiling water.

7

PURITY AND PUNISHMENT

For Muhammad's devoted and devout followers the Koran was not enough to cover all their legal, social and religious needs, so over a long period the "Traditions" came into being in the form of the Hadith, the great body of verbal and written accounts of the words and deeds of the Prophet and his companions. This led to the Sunna, the term for the entire theory and practice of the universal Islamic community. The other fundamental institution of Islam is the Shari'a, the civil and criminal law of Islam, partly taken from the 500 Koranic verses which refer to the legal points.

With the Koran itself, Hadith and Sunna and Shari'a are the basis of Muslim life. The Hadith traditions are particularly interesting in the way that they came into being, though historians accept a strictly limited number of Hadiths as truly representing the Prophet's thoughts. They are not authentic historical documents because they do not exist, and they were not set down in writing until two or three centuries after Muhammad's death. The person who reports a tradition states that he heard it from somebody else, and so on through a chain of men until we stretch back to a contemporary of Muhammad who saw something happen with his own eyes or heard it with his own ears. There is no guarantee of authenticity, nor can there be. The historical importance of the Hadiths is that they reveal aspects of the age in which they were invented and their durability shows something of Islamic belief in what is being stated. They are often contradictory, thus giving Muslims a wide latitude in their everyday code of conduct.

For many generations after Muhammad the great hunger for Hadiths resulted in their being fabricated by the thousand. Many were invented by students who could quickly build up their reputations by "discovering" Hadiths. Even aphorisms from Greek philosophy were put into the mouth of the Prophet. Men made long journeys for the sole aim of collecting Hadiths, without any understanding of their content, simply to allow the traveler to boast of them. As early as the second Islamic century a Muslim writer describes how an infamous Hadith inventor operated in a particular mosque. "If anyone had but offered him twopence he would have transmitted seventy Hadith in return." Several "great" inventors of Hadith said that they did so in order to turn people back to a study of the Koran.

The whole business cried out for rationalization, form and system and when this was achieved each "official" Hadith was prefaced by a chain of authorities going back to the original narrator. The process was called *isnad* (backing). This *isnad* appears in the standard Hadith collection formed by al-Bukhari: "It was told us by Abdallah ibn Ysuf who said, it was told us by al-Laith, who had it from Yazid, who had it from Abu'l-Khair, who had it from Uqba ibn Amir—He said . . ."

According to Muslim tradition, Bukhari examined more than 200,000 Hadiths—and rejected another 200,000 without examination. He selected as genuine about 7,300 but effectively there are only 2,762 as many are repeated in different contexts.

The great scholars criticize some Hadiths as being flagrantly opposed to the teaching of the Koran and so undignified as to have been impossible for the Prophet to have uttered. Examples include: "If it were permissible for mankind to bow down to anyone but God I would have commanded women to bow down before their husbands." And: "If anything is a bad omen it would be women and horses."

More acceptable Hadiths include:

Leave that which makes you doubt for that which does not make you doubt.

Part of someone's being a good Muslim is his leaving alone that which does not concern him.

If you feel no shame, then do as you wish.

The ink of the man of knowledge is more worthy than the blood of the martyr.

It is better to have a tyrannical government for a time than a period of revolution.

He who leaves the community by the [short] distance of only one span has cut himself off from Islam.

Hell has seven gates; one of them is destined for those who draw the sword upon my community.

Obey your superiors and resist not, for to obey them is to obey God, to rebel against them is to rebel against Allah.

Other Hadiths exhort the believers and comfort them by saying that if it is not possible to alter prevailing evil with hand and tongue it is sufficient to protest with the heart. "He who is an eyewitness and disapproves will be considered as if he had not seen it."

Certain Hadiths declare that the best of the Muslim community is he who contracts the most marriages. Celibacy is against the Sunna and except among the Sufi sect seems to be unknown in Islam. Another layer of Hadiths teaches that even a wicked government must be obeyed and that it must be left to Allah to cause the downfall of rulers of whom He disapproves.

In numerous Hadiths the Prophet talks of the supremacy of contemplation over action. Most Muslims have taken this to heart, as those Westerners who do business in Islamic countries know to their frustration. In Tripoli President Gaddafi once kept me waiting five weeks for an interview. All journalists have waited interminably for an official car to call for them, and know what little importance "appointments" have. The same lack of action applies in affairs of state. The Dutch Ambassador in Tripoli at the time I was waiting for Gaddafi commiserated with me—he had been kept waiting for six weeks to present his credentials.

Professor Gibb believes that the Islamic theologians could do a great service to Islam by determined action on the Hadiths—"ruthlessness in throwing out four-fifths of what passes for what Muhammad said." But he recognizes that this will take more than a century to accomplish.

Since Islam became a daily topic in newspapers outside Islam, one of the most frequently used words is Shari'a—the "clear path." While it is based on the Koran, it also is firmly rooted in the sayings and deeds of Muhammad and on the concensus of Islamic scholars. More than a framework of law as we in the West understand the word, the Shari'a is a complex, all-embracing code of ethics, morality and religious duties.

Islam has five "duties":

> Prayer.
> Fasting.
> Tithing, and the one-fifth. (The one fifth, or al-kums, is the paying to the community of 20 per cent of the spoils of war and, according to some sects, of proceeds from the treasures of the earth, such as minerals, as well as commercial earnings.)
> Struggle for the sake of Allah.
> Commending good deeds and forbidding evil ones.

Islam's traditional ethics are also divided into five categories—things commanded, things commended, things deplored, things prohibited—and a fifth classification to deal with actions which do not fit easily into the other four. We can describe this section as "miscellaneous," "neutral" or "overlapping."

Failing to fulfill some obligation and committing some prohibited act are severely censured while indulging in the deplored and neglecting the desirable are relatively censured.

Some latitude may exist in relation to duties and ethics but law is thought of as a matter of divine inspiration and therefore immutable: it is not, as in the West, the product of human intelligence and adaptation to changing social ideals and needs. In the West to ignore, flout or violate the Law is the equivalent of infringing a rule of social order. In Islam it goes beyond this; it is an act of religious disobedience, a *sin*. It therefore involves a religious penalty. As Gibb says, "The conception of Law in Islam is authoritarian to the last degree."

Islam forbids frivolous pleasures, singing and playing of musical instruments of any kind, gambling, liquor, slander, lying, meanness, coarseness, intrigue, treachery, calumny, disloyalty in friendship, disavowal of kinship, ill-nature, arrogance, boasting, sly scheming, haughtiness, insult and obscenity, spite and envy, inconstancy, aggressiveness and tyranny.

In some important Islamic societies a *muhtasib* or guardian of public morality used to be employed to maintain purity of the faith. He had to see that men did not consort with women in public and he was strict with people he caught playing musical instruments. Also, he had direct supervision over games and toys, for although they were not directly contrary to law they might be associated with causes of offense. For instance, dolls, which are lawful in encouraging the maternal instincts of girls, may lead to the portraiture of married women or the representation of idols. In some places dolls are still forbidden. In Saudi Arabia religious police with canes vigorously enforce the closing of shops so that the faithful are not kept from prayer.

Islamic legal doctrine does not operate on the basis of protecting the individual against the state; the jurists subordinate the principle of individual liberty to that of public interest and welfare. Under this "ideal form" of government, they argue, all men will naturally receive their due rights. But the Islamic scholar N. J. Coulson identifies a "supreme paradox" which nullifies this pious ideal. "It lies in the fact that the *Shari'a* fails to provide any guarantee that government will, in practice, assume this ideal form, and that, far from ensuring the existence of practical remedies against the ruler's abuse of his recognized powers, it simply counsels acceptance of such abuse."*

The jurists concede the power of the ruler to employ the use of threats or the extortion of confessions by corporal punishment and imprisonment, finding the necessary precedent in the practice of the early Islamic rulers. The Caliph 'Ali, it is said, to discover the truth of the plaintiff's claim that he had become dumb as the result of an assault, ordered that his tongue should be pierced with a needle; if red blood appeared the plaintiff was lying, but if the blood was black he was indeed dumb.

Where the normal rules of procedure are ineffective it seems that the ruler is allowed to adopt, "within reason," any method to discover the facts of the case. Particularly harsh treatment is recommended for the individual of reputedly bad character whose guilt is suspected but cannot be proved. He should be subjected to rigorous interrogation, with beating and imprisonment if necessary, for as the jurist Tabsirat states, "Were we simply to subject each suspect to the oath and then free him, in spite of our knowledge of his notoriety in crime, saying: 'We cannot convict him without two witnesses,' that would be contrary to good law." Should the suspect be released there is no question of a case for malicious prosecution or false imprisonment. It is only where no proof is forthcoming and the person charged is of such high repute that none would normally suspect him of the alleged offense that the accuser will be punished.

The law differs from country to country depending on which of four major schools of interpretation—Hanafi, Maliki, Shafei and Hanbali—is followed. But in all schools judges opt for severity rather than leniency in case of doubt. An American couple newly posted to Saudi Arabia caught their Pakistani houseboy stealing and ordered him to report to the police, expecting him to be reprimanded. They were appalled and astonished when he

*The International and Comparative Law Quarterly, January 1957.

returned home minus a hand. It had been chopped off and the stub of his arm plunged into boiling tallow to disinfect it.*

Supposedly, a thief who is poor, "in need" or mentally sick is not punished. A father stealing from his son is also not at risk and boys are not punished by hand amputation; a Libyan scholar told me, "If we cut off the hands of boy thieves, by the time that generation grew up we would find that most men were one-handed!"

In North Yemen a convicted thief is required to pick up his chopped-off hand and raise it to his head as a salute to the presiding judge.

The Western public was shocked in January 1978 when the execution of the lovely Princess Misha was disclosed. Misha, aged only nineteen, had been reluctantly married to a much older cousin, who had left her. An accomplished dancer, vivacious and fun-loving, Misha fell in love with a handsome young Saudi and met him sometimes in London, despite the strict security imposed by her grandfather, Prince Muhammad Bin Abdul; the womenfolk were not supposed to be allowed out without two men employees watching them. Misha tried to fake her own death by drowning and then escape from Saudi Arabia but somebody betrayed her and like many lesser Saudis, Misha was stoned to death and her lover was beheaded.

In a case with which I am familiar in Saudi Arabia four men were convicted of rape. One, a bachelor, was beheaded. The other three were married and therefore guilty of adultery as well as rape. They were buried up to the waist in sand and stoned to death by a mob that used small rocks instead of big ones, to prolong their agony. Stoning is a social event because in the eyes of Islam the adulterer has been guilty of a crime against the whole of society.

Sometimes the victims pay too. When a German girl was raped by two men in Saudi Arabia in 1977 the judge ordered her flogged "as an accomplice to immorality."†

---

*Time, July 25, 1977.
†Yet, according to 'Abd al-Qasir as-Sufi, in his book Jihad—A Ground Plan, the "Shari'a is compassionate, generous and lenient."

His reasoning was that as she was not covered from head to toe—she was wearing an ordinary Western dress—she must have provided a degree of "incitement." It is rare for a raped woman to escape blame for what has befallen her.

According to the law, for adultery to be proven the act must be witnessed by four adult males. Also, it is not rare for a group of men, denied the favors of some woman, to fabricate evidence against her and against a rival whom they suspect she has favored. A Muslim Islamic expert on a BBC program, "Nation to Nation," in March 1979 made a significant comment: "Any man who is caught practicing adultery in such a position as to be seen by four witnesses is not a man who is practicing his own personal liberty but someone who is affecting the whole social value of society." This seems to imply that adulterers are being punished mainly for allowing themselves to be observed.

Englishmen and Frenchmen who have served time in Saudi prisons for selling liquor to Muslims have described conditions as barbaric. Prisoners are allowed no exercise, no privacy and most sleep on thin foam mattresses, about fifteen men to a cell that measures five meters square. The staple diet is chicken and rice which, to a Westerner, is virtually inedible. Toilet facilities are primitive. Western prisoners report seeing Arabs, found guilty of unspecified crimes, being trussed up in leg and arm irons and lowered into holes in the ground where they remain for weeks on end, food and water being passed to them twice a day.

Puritanical conservatism is no longer confined to Saudi Arabia and Libya. Even the once tolerant Gulf states have a whole new series of punishments—forty lashes for Muslims who drink, sell or manufacture alcohol, amputation of the right hand for thieves and of the left leg for second offenders, 100 lashes for unmarried adulterers and public stoning to death for their married partners.

Even Egypt, with the most cosmopolitan capital in the Muslim world, has recently reintroduced the Shari'a laws, including the death penalty for any Muslim-Egyptian guilty of apostasy—renouncing his religion. When I was in Egypt in 1973 upper-class Cairenes were talking of the recent murders of a Christian priest and two Muslims he had converted. No action was taken to find the killers.

Is Islamic law a deterrent? The Saudis think so and say that their crime rate is one of the lowest in the world. But recently an influx of low-income foreign workers, most of them Muslim, has caused an upsurge in crime, suggesting that knowing the laws of the Shari'a and awareness that they are enforced is not necessarily a deterrent.

One great and welcome change which has taken place in parts of the Islamic world—Malaysia and Indonesia among them—is the institution of courts of appeal. The Shari'a knows of no such courts and they are therefore an innovation.

Unhappily, against this enlightened reform we must set the increasing frequency of men being charged with offenses against Allah or against religion. Hundreds have been so accused since Khomeini's revolution in Iran. The charge is regarded as so heinous that it practically precludes defense and the penalty is always death. Few lawyers will run the risk of appearing for a man accused of crimes against religion because inevitably they arouse the anger of the religious judges.

The great German Islamic scholar, C. H. Becker, has defined more clearly than anybody else a phenomenon concerning the Shari'a that many observers have felt. "In the traditional Muslim world the individual feels a special respect for the Shari'a even if he does not know what it is. Thus he conceives the whole of his life as bound round with a network of obligations, all regulated by religion. This leads him to give a sacred character to all existing institutions, even those that have no Islamic origin. Such an attitude must produce an uncritical conservatism which prevents experiment and innovation."*

Becker is indicating the West and the Christian world's point of departure from Islam. It is this "uncritical conservatism" which we most need to fear, because it cannot compromise. The Westerner who mentions the benefits of democracy or suggests the need for a constitution is told that nothing of the kind is necessary in Islam; what need

*Islamstudien, Berlin, 1959.

has any Muslim state of any more laws and statutes when it has the Holy Koran and the Traditions?

Western societies have long since reformed themselves, or tried to do so, and the process is continual. There have been gross aberrations, as in the Nazi period in Germany, and in modern times in certain South American countries and in South Africa. But forces are constantly at work, even within the most ruthless police states, vigorously denouncing bad law and, in the end, bringing about reform. Even the beginning of this process is barely visible in Islam.

In some ways Islam shows a great gulf between principle and practice. According to Mawdudi and other Muslims Islam provided the first rules "to make war civilized and humane." Mawdudi invokes sayings by the Prophet which regulate the rights of combatants. For instance, "Do not attack a wounded person," an injunction which Mawdudi takes to mean that wounded soldiers who are unfit to fight, and are not actually fighting, should not be attacked. Similarly, the Prophet said, "No prisoner should be put the sword," and he prohibited the killing of anyone who is tied up or is in captivity. Most importantly, the Prophet insisted that no old person, nor any child or any woman should be killed. A Hadith further states "The Prophet has prohibited us from mutilating the corpses of the enemies," and another Hadith is to the effect that corpses of fallen warriors must be handed back to their people.

These are fine, humane principles but they have been disobeyed on countless occasions. An interesting phenomenon is that many Muslim historians—Mawdudi is a classic modern example—insist that Muslims have not and do not behave in a barbaric manner when sober History shows that they have done so again and again. Numerous prosaic accounts in English, French, Dutch, Italian, Spanish and other languages tell of captured wounded being slaughtered out of hand, of captives tortured and corpses mutilated at Muslim hands. Captured Israeli soldiers have been bound hand and foot with wire before being shot to death; I have photographs of them. The killers on one occasion known to me were Syrian

Muslims.* The Egyptians often decapitated Muslim prisoners and corpses during the war against Yemen in 1966. During the Iranian Revolution of 1979 some prisoners were torn to pieces by mobs.

---

*No historian would claim that Muslims are the only cruel soldiers. Most armies were guilty of atrocities in the past and some have committed them in modern times—the German Nazis, the Russians, the Japanese for example. But even they did not claim to be following "humane and civilized" principles while ignoring those very principles.

8

AL-AZHAR—
ISLAMIC POLICY CENTER

Islam as a whole gets its direction and has its standards reinforced from al-Azhar, the great university and religious institute in Cairo. All Muslim countries with the exception of Turkey pay attention to the pronouncements which emanate from al-Azhar because this ancient center of Islamic scholarship—it was built in 969 and claims to be the oldest university in the world—makes "official" policy.

Much of this policy evolves from periodic conferences of the Islam Research Academy held at al-Azhar and attended by the leading theologians from most Muslim countries. The great majority of these men are middle-aged to elderly and they tend to be fundamentalists.

Almost without exception the papers presented are austere in tone, militant in content, and authoritative and unequivocal in intent. Intention is vitally important in Islam and on one particular gate at al-Azhar is the inscription, "Truly, actions are judged by their intention and every man is rewarded by what he intended." This saying of the Prophet is considered to be one of the most important principles of Islam; theologians apply it to their treatment of religious and legal questions. The intention of the theologians who spend their lives at al-Azhar and those dignitaries who visit from time to time is to be obeyed.

A vast amount of material issues from al-Azhar and by Western academic standards the documents are repetitive and prolix. It is possible here to give only brief examples. In some cases the first or last sentence sums up an argument which may take many pages. For instance, in 1976 Sheikh Abdel Halim Mahmud, Grand Imam of the University, announced that "Stealing will completely disappear if the thief's hand is cut off." He supported this with heavy quotation from Islamic law and experience.

In October 1968, at the fourth conference of the Islamic Research Academy, Sheikh Muhammad Zahra announced: "To hug or kiss a girl is a crime." He went on to explain that hugging and kissing could lead to the even worse crimes of fornication and adultery. Sheikh Zahra was one of Islam's foremost theologians so his pronouncement had to be taken seriously. It is impossible for any person in the West to assess the impact of his virtual proscription of hugging and kissing but it must at least have had the effect of further inhibiting relations between the sexes.

The examples of Islamic theological argument which follow are taken from the Academy's fourth conference in 1968.*

On Jihad

Sheikh Abdullah Ghoshah, Supreme Judge of the Hashemite Kingdom of Jordan, in presenting a paper on Jihad, made some significant revelations.

Jihad is legislated in order to be one of the means of propagating Islam. Consequently non-Muslims ought to embrace Islam either willingly or through wisdom and good advice or unwillingly through fight

*Some of the proceedings were reproduced immediately after the conference in the university's monthly magazine. The complete transactions were published in 1970 in Arabic (3 vols.) and in English (1 volume, 935 pages). The publisher was the Egyptian Government Printing Office, which sought no copyright.

and jihad. Scholars lay the foundation of the foreign policy of the Islamic states on the following bases:

1. It is unlawful to give up Jihad and adopt peace and weakness, unless the purpose of giving up is for preparation, whenever there is something weak among Muslims and their opponents are strong.

2. War is the basis of the relationship between Muslims and their opponents unless there are justifiable reasons for peace such as adopting Islam or making an agreement with them to keep peaceful.

3. The abode of Islam is the homeland which is subject to the rules of Islam . . . The abode of war is the nation which is not subject to the rules of Islam . . .

4. Muslims are free to break their covenant with enemies if they are uneasy lest the enemies should betray them . . .

The Sheikh quoted two traditional authorities on Islam. From Al Tabarani: "Lies are sins except when they are told for the welfare of a Muslim or for saving him from disaster." From Ibn Al Arabi: "Telling lies in war is permitted so as to comfort the Muslims when they are in need of it as in the time of fighting."

Sheikh Ghoshah concluded his address with an observation on arrogance: "Allah, the Almighty, loves the Muslim to be arrogant when he is fighting as it manifests that he is indifferent to his enemy and that he determines to vanquish him."

Sheikh Zahra supported Ghoshah:

Jihad is not confined to the summoning of troops and the establishment of huge forces. It takes various forms. From all the territories of Islam there should arise a group of people reinforced with faith, well equipped with means and methods; and then let them set out to attack the usurpers, harassing them incessantly until their abode is one of everlasting torment . . . Jihad will never end . . . it will last to the Day of Judgment. But war comes to a close as far as a particular group of people are concerned. It is terminated when the war aims are realized, either by the repulse of aggression and the enemy's surrender by the signing of a covenant or by permanent peace treaty or truce.

On Islam
Hassan Khaled, Mufti of the Lebanese Republic:

Our today's Islamic society is one of disconnected limbs, shattered body and dissolving character. In it intoxicants are sold, usury is swallowed down, indecencies prevail, the modesties of women are raped and the holy sanctities violated. We, the so-called Muslims . . . who know Allah and who are supposed to be religious commit those sins. They are more sinful and more notorious than others.

On Jews
The conference was held only a year after the Six-Day War, in which Israel had been victorious, so the Jews were a major topic and many delegates spoke against them. His Eminence, the Grand Imam, Rector of al-Azhar University, said:

It is inconceivable that Allah would grant to the Unbelievers a way to triumph over the Believers. For this reason the setback that has befallen us is nothing but a sign of Allah's solicitude for our welfare since we have, certainly, the genuine sentiment of religion, even if we have missed the ways of the pious . . . We ulama (religious leaders) have also to make clear to the Islamic peoples that the lingering spirit of the past Crusades that was utterly routed by the feats of valor and heroic resistance of our forefathers, had made of the present-day Zionism a spearhead launched against Muslims by the enemies of humanity and advocates of imperialism . . .

Several speakers stated that it was outrageous for the Jews, traditionally kept by Arab Islam in a humiliated inferior status and characterized as cowardly, to defeat the Arabs, have their own state and cause the "contraction of the abode of Islam." All these events contradicted the design of Allah and the march of History.

Professor Abdul Sattar El Sayed, the Mufti of Tursos, Syria, told the conference that according to the Koran the Jews were an enemy without any human feelings.

On apostasy

Sheikh Abu Zahra demanded death for apostates.

No one who professes a faith would ever think of abjuring it unless he discovers the falsity of its tenets, no believer ever thinks of rejecting it except under compulsion . . . Most apostates from Islam have only been opportunists who adopt Islam for worldly purposes and having achieved their selfish ends relapse into their former faith. Such opportunists want only to adopt the faith without any serious intent. A severe punishment must be inflicted on apostates so that whoever embraces Islam should know the penalty once he deflects therefrom. And there is no doubt that anyone who enters a place, knowing that he is going to be shut within, will think twice before entering . . . Islam is the law of the Muslim state. Whoever trifles with it is only seeking to upset the organic law of the state. It is right that the state should protect its system with the most severe penalties, seeing that an apostate is a rebel against the state, who deserves the utmost punishment.

This speech by Abu Zahra makes quite clear the indivisibility of religion and politics in Islam.

The increasing importance of al-Azhar and similar institutes established in Saudi Arabia and Pakistan and in Europe has given the Islamic priesthood more influence.

Islam is said to have no priesthood and classically this is so; it was feared that members of a priesthood might claim a right to intervene between God and man. But to deny the existence of a religious profession or a clergy is to split hairs; there is a class with exclusively religious functions—the leaders of prayer, the mosque officials, preachers at prayer services, judges and theologians. Mullahs, ayatollahs, imams—there is a long list of titles covering the many countries—have assumed the role of priest in giving spiritual counsel and theological advice. In the countryside the imam of the mosque is often the teacher of elementary education and is the arbiter of most disputes. Ayatollahs are expected to know what is best for the public on any issue and, in Iran at least, each ayatollah can interpret the law according to the situation he faces. In the first two decades of this century in country after country—Morocco, Algeria, Tunisia, Libya, Egypt, Syria, Iraq and Indonesia—the national movement was led and often created by religious groups.

With the coming of independence the "clergy" has been rising in the social scale and in influence. This is understandable. Independence and then power, through oil or any other commodity, are indications that History is getting back onto the right track, that Allah is at least beginning to look benignly on Islam and at last starting to forgive Muslims for whatever wrong they committed in the past. Since the clergy are interpreters of Allah, they are given considerably more respect by the faithful in this new situation. If some mullah or ayatollah or imam can promise the people "progress" and *if they believe him* they will follow him. Khomeini did not make the mistake of promising to get rid of poverty and squalor—a good many Iranians draw their security from their poverty and squalor. The luckless Shah saw progress in terms of concrete and chrome and housing developments, and permissiveness. He went too far too fast.

The strength of the theologians of al-Azhar and of the mullahs far removed from the centers of learning is that they do *not* offer progress; they stand for stability and security based on the ancient tenets of Islam. One of the most attractive of Islam's offers is certainty of belief.

An American scholar, Raphael Patai, expresses the same point in another way. "Under traditional Islam efforts at human improvement have rarely transcended ineffectuality. Dominated by Islam, the Arab mind has been bent more on preserving than innovating, on maintaining than improving, on continuing than initiating"*

The fundamentalist theologians have broken a way into modern politics through the Shari'a. This was a well chosen point of entry. Because of the central religious significance of the Shari'a it has been difficult even for powerful modernizing Muslims—the Shah, President Sadat and Mr. Bhutto—to oppose fundamentalists' demands on law. These leaders used the traditional Muslim subterfuge of accepting the zealots' ideas in principle while doing nothing about them in practice. Refusing to be fobbed off, the zealots returned to the attack with claims that there should be Islamic control over the Constitution and over legislation. And they have won their demands everywhere.

*The Arab Mind, Charles Scribner's Sons, New York, 1973.

9

ISLAM AND CHRISTIANITY

Fully to understand Islam as a life force Christians need to visit the port of Jedda, Saudi Arabia, and see the arrival of multitudes of pilgrims on the way to Mecca. At least two million each year are making the pilgrimage or Hajj. It would be even more impressive to see the Muslims in their religious devotions in Mecca, but the city is forbidden to non-Muslims.

Every Muslim is expected to make the Hajj at least once. The journey can be long, arduous and expensive; some Muslims in far places save all their lives to make the trip, which takes place in the month of Thil-Hijjah, the twelfth lunar month of the Muslim calendar. On the tenth day of the month the blessed feast of al-Adhha (the Sacrifice), a festival of prayer and dedication to Allah, begins.

Most of the millions of pilgrims will live in tents on the arid plains of Arafat, near Mecca, and perform the exhausting and complex week-long ritual of feast and prayer. Divested of all their regular clothes and ornaments, they dress in two white sheets. There is no distinction between rich and poor, black and white, Arab or non-Arab, male or female. All are equal, all must abstain from sexual intercourse. They perform unified religious rituals and all repeat together, "Yes (ready, obedience) my Lord, yes! Thou has no partner! Yes!" Then they offer their animal sacrifices and much blood is shed by throat-cutting. Thousands of sacrificial sheep and goats are kept ready by the Bedouins and merchants and prices are high. Only people of high rank slaughter camels. The pilgrim who does not care to kill the animal himself may pay a butcher to do it. It is considered meritorious to give the flesh of the slain animals to the poor; what they do not use is left lying. The sacrifice is celebrated on this day throughout the Muslim world, but feasting can be substituted for sacrifice.

Since he is unable to go to Mecca, the Islamic life force is more easily visible for a non-Muslim if he watches the worshippers at some great mosque anywhere in the world, as Muslims go through the ritual washing at the specially provided taps and then enter the mosque for prayer. Some mosques are vast, cool and cavernous places—such as the main mosque in Damascus. The sense of sanctuary is strong, even for a non-Muslim, and especially when it is not being visited by throngs of tourists. Superstitions are attached to certain mosques; that connected to a pair of columns in the mosque of 'Amr in Old Cairo is well known; only true believers can squeeze through the gap and many people flock to the miraculous columns, particularly after the noon service of the last Friday in Ramadan in order to prove their virtue.

Islam has a formal simplicity within the mosque. Worshippers take off their shoes before entering a mosque but no special garments are worn by anybody, there is no incantation, no solemn music, no choir, no ritual involving the central importance of the "minister." The imam occupies the minbar, a type of pulpit, and sets the time for the sequence of movements, but any ordinary man can lead the prayers. All present are participants all the time, never passive spectators. All perform the praying movements rhythmically and together, all use the identical words.

It is during the holy month of Ramadan that the Islamic life force is put to its greatest test. Ramadan is the only month to be mentioned by name in the Koran—as the month in which the Holy Book was "sent down." It is supposed to be a time of intensified devotion and mutual forgiveness; in practice it is a rigorous discipline and ordeal which has no parallel in Christian and Jewish experience. For twenty-eight days there is an absolute prohibition of all bodily sustenance by whatever means during daylight hours—it is an "offense" to swallow your own spittle in some Islamic countries—and an abstinence from sexual activity. The ban on drinking imposes great hardship when it occurs in summer—the Muslim year follows the lunar calendar so Ramadan "moves." Trade and industry are largely at a standstill, especially in the hot season. People are inclined to make up during the night for the deprivations of the day. As sleeping is not forbidden during the fast, they often sleep a part of the day; the night is given up to all sort of pleasures and many people gorge themselves as a way of balancing their daily starvation. Smokers listen with rapt attention to the radio so that when the end of the day's abstinence is officially announced, often by a cannon shot, they can light up at once.

Except during Ramadan or some other special occasion non-Muslims fail to notice or ignore the fact that Islam, unlike Christianity, has retained its predominance in daily life throughout the Islamic lands. Having reached a stage of social development where religion is seen more in moral values than theological precepts, most Western visitors to Islamic countries come to believe that the educated classes have accepted a liberal Western attitude towards religion. This mistake is easily made because many educated Muslims speak European languages, dress like Westerners, frequently visit Western countries and in many cases have had Western education. Those Europeans who have come to know Muslims in the West and later meet them in their homeland are often astonished at the difference. The casual, free and easy manner so evident in New York, London or Paris has vanished; their Muslim friends have reverted to the Islamic model, with all the formality and rigidity which this implies.

Muslim religious observances are in no way a threat to the West but their quietly passionate intensity is indicative of an Islamic attitude and state of mind.

Total involvement in his religion—the "surrender"

which is the very meaning of Islam—both prevents the Muslim from wanting to know much about other religions and makes him hostile to them. Any book which sets out to describe the "dagger of Islam," largely for a Western public, must explain Islam's attitude to Christianity. It is equally a "must" that Christian political leaders—whether they are themselves religious or not—understand these attitudes and the problems they cause. Such knowledge may obviate difficulties.

One statesman well aware of Muslim ignorance about Christianity was Dr. Charles Malik, a Prime Minister of Lebanon and a former Lebanese Ambassador to the United Nations. Writing in *Foreign Affairs* in 1952, Dr. Malik said:

> There is an amazing ignorance of Christian literature, doctrine and life, despite the fact that Christ and his Mother are deeply revered by Islam. There isn't a single Muslim scholar in all history, so far as I know, who has written an authentic essay on Christianity; whereas Christian scholars, both Arab and non-Arab, have written authoritative works on Islam and on other religions too . . . There will always be fear, uncertainty, embarrassment, uneasiness, lack of joy, lack of freedom, and a predisposition to self-defense until this spiritual and intellectual imbalance is redressed.

The attitudes so well known to Malik indicate the superiority with which Muslims hold their system of belief in comparison with other faiths. Christians and Jews whose families had lived under Islam for centuries constantly had to find ways of protecting themselves and their practices against it.

Islam claims to accept Christianity and in principle this may be so, but the scholar Albert Hourani, highly regarded in the Arab world, rejects this claim in modern times. "The tolerance which the present-day Muslim professes for Christians . . . is too often not that of a humble believer for those whom he recognizes as serious seekers of the same truth, but contemptuous toleration of the strong for the weak."*

Hourani also says that Orthodox Muslims are "uneasy in the presence of Christianity" because Christianity can only be understood as part of a process which culminates in the coming of Muhammad—yet Christians reject Muhammad.

One difficulty is that Muhammad's character and personality seem very different from that which Christians would expect to find in a prophet. He built a kingdom by the use of power and violence. For this reason, if for no other, Islam could not be thought of as carrying further and completing the Christian message.

For their part, Muslims regard Christians as infidels and because they do not accept some of Muhammad's teaching they are described as "people of low intelligence." They do not possess the mental capacity to break away from the routine thinking which imprisons them. The Koranic references are numerous—3:58/63 and 102/103; 10:42/43; 22:45/46; 59:14.

Muslims also know from the Koran that Allah detests those people who are not willing to re-examine their fundamental ideas; they are among the worst people of all (8:23; 10:100). This is ironic, since Islam as a system, and Muslims as members of that system, are almost totally unself-critical.

To the Muslim, the Christian concept of a God who became man and, while man, suffered and died, smacks of blasphemy, while the Catholic veneration of statues of Christ, Mary and the saints is idolatrous. The orthodox Muslim belief is that Jesus did not die on the Cross; either someone was crucified in his place—Judas, perhaps—or he was crucified but escaped death.

Muslims do not relate to God in the sense of "Father and children" or "Pastor and flock," as in the Christian concept. God is so exalted, so total, that mere mortal men cannot approach him. In the same way Islam is less interested in the spiritual comfort of man than it is about the tremendous omnipotence of God.

---

*Minorities in the Arab World, Oxford University Press, 1947.

It is possible for Christians to accept elements of Islam such as belief in One God who has spoken to man, in judgment, in Jesus regarded as a prophet. These are perhaps enough on which to build a harmonious relationship and the Vatican Council in 1965 with some difficulty but much sincerity defined a Christian attitude towards Islam.* But Christians must be cautious since it is the way of Islamic people to regard tolerance and humility as weaknesses.

Islamic fanatics will not accept that the Vatican is sincere; and as-Sufi and other accuse it, along with the World Council of Churches, of systematically "corrupting Islam." For as-Sufi, Islam is under attack from several quarters. "Clearly," he says, "Islam is politically and culturally an alien nomadic force, an embattled minority, an endangered species." Even states considered rigidly Islamic in the West, such as Saudi Arabia and Libya, are betrayers of Islam according to as-Sufi. The adoption of slogans on human rights, especially by the "ignorant Saudi leaders," is a sign that they do not believe in the Shari'a—since such rights are not specifically mentioned in the Shari'a.

as-Sufi wants no Ministers of Islamic Affairs because the existence of such a cabinet post implies that there is some division between Islamic Affairs and everything else that goes on in an Islamic state. Especially as-Sufi wants to end any attempt to set up what he terms "an Islamic vatican" in Mecca. The Islamic Secretariat, he says, "a masonically designed body . . . is the most powerful and insidious enemy of Islam" because it confirms nationalism; as-Sufi wants a supra-national Islamic religious community not an international political one.†

The elimination of poverty is a "demented Christian thesis," according to as-Sufi, but even much less extreme critics make forthright comments about Western Christian behavior. Dr. Said Adash, an Egyptian imam at the Muslim Cultural Center, London, told a BBC interviewer in March, 1979, that "If the West were a proper Chris-

*Vatican Council: Concile oecumenique Vatican II: documentes consiliares. Paris, 1965, p. 215.
†Op. cit. Jihad—a Groundplan.

tian society we would feel happier in our dealings with the West. We reject the decadent way of life in Western society ... [as] anti-Christian, [with its] drinking, permissiveness ... pornography ... ."

Raphael Patai interprets Muslim attitudes as an apprehension. "What Muslims fear from Westernization is not that it will cause their co-religionists to abandon Islam in favor of Christianity but that it will bring about a reduction of the function of Islam to the modest level on which Christianity plays its role in the Western world."

Christians living within the Muslim world face much more than verbal hostility. In Syria adherence to Islam became so manifestly a condition of citizenship that Christians were driven out on the grounds that they were not citizens. This trend began in 1955 when the Prime Minister himself, Faris al-Khuri, was a Christian. A popular Imam in Damascus publicly declared that Indonesian Muslims were closer to him than his own Syrian Christian Prime Minister. This was tantamount to a political death sentence for al-Khuri, and since that time no Christian has served in a high political capacity. Each administration has become increasingly nationalistic, anti-Western and pragmatically pro-Communist. The absence of any legal or judicial guarantees for the Christians and other minorities has revived old fears and apprehensions. Many politically motivated Syrian Christians either have emigrated or accept secondary positions within the existing system. The Christians of Iraq have been doing a knife-edge balancing act since 1963 when Muslim reaction following the overthrow of General Kassem forced about 35,000 of them to flee from their homes in Mosul, Tall Kayf and other villages to the relative safety of Baghdad. Now the leaders of the Christian community refrain from public reference to religious inequalities for fear of precipitating Muslim reaction. "Incidents" are numerous but the Christian leaders manage to paper over most of them. Occasionally they are helpless, as in August 1966 when a Syrian Christian pilot, Colonel Munir Rufa'a, fled with his Soviet MIG-21 to Israel. He told the world that he had sought asylum in Israel to escape the religious intolerance to which he as a Christian was subjected in Muslim Iraq. The Iraqi Christians were harassed for years because of Colonel Rufa'a's indiscreet comments.

In Iran, too, anti-Christian feeling has not been far beneath the surface since Khomeini's revolution began in January, 1979. In February 1979 gunmen forced their way into the office of the Reverend P. Sayyah, the Iranian pastor of the Episcopal Church and shot him to death. Muslim extremists consider that the 2,000 members of the Iranian Christian Church are apostates. The Bazargan administration deplored the murder and described it as an isolated incident. This description is meaningless since the murder of a single pastor in a community of only 2,000 is enough to terrorize every person in it. The attack only needed to be "isolated" from the Islamic point of view. Two Christian churches closed when it became unsafe for British missionaries and volunteer English helpers and they returned home. Church income dropped drastically, so that the church's charitable and social work was cut.

In Pakistan in April 1979 Muslim mobs burnt an All Saints Church and attacked its pastor. This happened during a violent pro-Bhutto demonstration so it was particularly mindless as Christians had nothing but sympathy for Mr. Bhutto. But the instinctive action of many a Muslim mob is to attack Christian institutions.

It is commendable in Christian terms for leaders of the Western Christian world to call for more "dialogue" between Christians and Muslims—as the Archbishop of Canterbury, Dr. Coggan, did in March 1979. "It is essential for the two religions to understand each other better, and I pray for a closer relationship," said Dr. Coggan. He can be sure that no Islamic theologian will join him in this prayer. To understand Christians is, logically enough by Islamic terms, not Muslim ambition.

Each year some Christians adopt Islam for purposes of political, social or economic advancement, to obtain an easy divorce or because they feel that they will be physically safer as Muslims. It is easy enough for a Christian to become Muslim but the converse is difficult and dangerous. The writer on Islam, Stanley Morrison, noted that

"Nothing excites the fanaticism of the Muslim masses more than the word *tabshir*—'the preaching of the Gospel'—or word that a Muslim has been baptized."*

In the matter of winning converts Christianity could not have failed more ignominiously; some authorities say that not more than 2,000 Muslims have embraced Christianity in the last century. Conversely, Islam has won and is winning many converts from among Christians. A number of African political leaders who were Christians or pagans have adopted the faith of the Prophet, among them the former Emperor Bokassa of the Central African Empire and President Bongo of Gabon. Their reasons are more tactical than religious; a Muslim leader has a much better chance than a non-Muslim of getting his hands on dollars paid for oil and then recycled into the international economy. An enormous fund of petro-dollars can be tapped by a convert who appeals for money on the grounds of Islamic unity.

*"Arab Nationalism and Islam," *Middle East Journal*, April 1948.

10

ISLAM VS. THE WEST'S "INTELLECTUAL HAVOC"

Islam's more political and general attitude to Western society needs to be studied separately from its religious response. The two can never be entirely divided but as religion and politics are separate fields in Western thinking it is useful to look at Muslim political and social criticism of the West where this is more or less specific.

The West set the pace of the relationship. No sooner had it established contact with the Islamic world towards the end of the eighteenth century than it began to study its history, religion, literature, and every other manifestation of Islamic culture. Before long Western Arabists or Orientalists knew more about these matters than the best local scholars themselves. If these scholars wanted to make a serious scientific study of their own history, religion or literature they had to start by reading the books written by the Western researchers. This hurt Arab pride. And what they read sometimes hurt them even more. The most unpalatable lesson was that with the end of the Middle Ages the Muslim Arabs had sunk into a stagnation and that they remained in it until awakened by the West.

For two centuries generations of religious leaders observed, with feelings ranging from unease to desperation, the percolation of Western ideas. Relentlessly and steadily they seeped through in literature and education, administration and commerce and intermingling brought about by conquest and travel. In one way or another the life of every Muslim was affected while the theologians could only watch in frustrated bitterness.

Muslim resentment, especially in the Arab lands, built up more steadily and intensely than Western politicians, church leaders, merchants and administrators ever suspected. Among the few Western people who understood the depth of Muslim animosity were the British naval officers and other officials charged with stopping the Arab trade in African Negro slaves.

Anti-Western sentiment became stronger in the period 1920–50 and various uprisings against imperial rule occurred. Ambitious young Muslims with political leanings joined illegal organizations and plotted revolutions against the occupying powers. One of them was Anwar Sadat, who was a member of the rightist pro-German Egyptian Youth Organization in 1940–41. From 1954 to 1961 he was secretary general of the Islamic Congress, which proposed to create close relations between Egypt and the Muslim countries of Asia and Africa. In one of his books, *Story of Arab Unity* (Cairo, 1957), he rejects Western civilization on the grounds that it dominated weaker nations through the exploitation of religion, science and ethics. For Sadat the evacuation of Egypt in 1956 by French, British and Israeli forces was a victory of the East over the West; he chooses to ignore the crucial role of the United States in forcing this evacuation.

Attacking the West for its materialism and ignorance, Sadat says that "Western civilization and its heritage, for which Europe and America fear so much, live only on the debris of the East and would not flourish if they had not sucked its blood."

This might seem to be extravagant language, but Sadat continues, "Democracy is a Western system designed to ensure Western authority and domination over the people of the East." In this comment he illustrates perhaps the most confusing aspect of Muslim comments about the West—Islam's opinions about what constitutes democracy. To Western peoples it means above all an elected government from a choice of parties and candidates. Islam claims to be democratic—yet in all Arab Islam and most of the rest of the Islamic world this system does not exist. There is no "popular" vote, no secrecy in voting, no ballot box. The majority of governments are in power by coup and some are absolute monarchies.

The differences between the two "democracies" have been explained by Mawlana Abdul A'la Mawdudi, regarded within Islam* as one of its greatest thinkers.

Mawdudi wrote:†

Of course what distinguishes Islamic democracy from Western democracy is that while the latter is based on the concept of popular sovereignty the former rests on the principle of popular *khalifa* [leadership]. In Western democracy, the people are sovereign, in Islam sovereignty is vested in God and the people are His caliphs or representatives. In the former the people make their own laws; in the latter they have to follow and obey the laws given by God through His Prophet. In one the government undertakes to fulfil the will of the people; in the other the government and the people who form it have all to fulfil the purpose of God. In brief, Western democracy is a kind of absolute authority which exercises its powers in a free and uncontrolled manner whereas Islamic democracy is subservient to the Divine law and exercises its authority in accordance with the injunctions of God and within the limits prescribed by Him.

This definition-by-contrast is illuminating since it cogently sums up the shortcomings of Western democracy as seen by Muslims.

Mawdudi not only attacks Western democracy; he is even more critical of the West's concept of the "right to

---

*And outside Islam. W. Cantwell Smith considers Mawdudi "much the most important systematic thinker of modern Islam." *Islam in Modern History*, Princeton, 1957.

†*Human Rights in Islam*, published by The Islamic Foundation, Leicester, 1976.

live." This right, he claims, has been given to man only by Islam. Not many nations have mentioned human rights in their Constitution or Declaration, Mawdudi states, but if they have done so then such rights are intended only for the white race. "This can clearly be gleaned from the fact that human beings were hunted down like animals in Australia and the land was cleared of aborigines for the white man." This allegation will not endear Mr. Mawdudi to the Australians; no historian has ever suggested that they hunted down the aborigines like animals.

Professing Muslims have written a vast amount in defense of their faith and in counter-attacking their "opponents." It would be difficult to deny that these works are inspired by loyalty and sincerity but it is equally difficult to find amid them anything which, as Professor Gibb expresses it, "appreciates the issues and meets them on the level of *current* thought." (My italics)

While Muslim academics deeply resent criticism from the West they never tire of telling their audiences about the decadence of the West and its inferiority to Islam—a habit which most Western-trained psychologists would recognize as a symptom of an inferiority complex or possibly that of a superiority complex.

Muslim politicians and intellectuals also often complain of being misrepresented. Foreign politicians might be guilty of this on occasions and journalists in a hurry are sometimes at fault but to condemn academic Orientalists, as a group, of failing to be truthful and accurate is surely an indication of hypersensitivity. The Iranian Professor Seyyed Nasr, who writes about the West in a scholarly way which demands to be accepted, nevertheless complains of "the willful misrepresentations of Islam by many Orientalists whose works have played no small part in wreaking intellectual havoc among many modernized Muslims."*

But such a charge can hardly be made against William R. Brown, dean of the School of Arts and Sciences of Central Connecticut State College, and an authority on Islam. Brown sees several sharp contrasts between West-

*Islam and the Plight of Modern Man, Longman, 1975.

erners and Muslims. Muslims, for instance, do not approach politics in our terms "because they have difficulty in identifying with the state in the same way we do or in contributing to the common but impersonal objectives of the government which embodies that state. . . . Muslims have not developed a strong sense of what we call 'civic responsibility'. . . . Their society seems to lack cohesiveness . . . the forces of social integration for which we strive."*

The Islam-West chasm is illustrated by Mawlana Mawdudi who elsewhere in his book claims that the Islamic conception of freedom of expression is "much superior" to the concept in the West. Yet in many Islamic countries the Press is either directed or heavily censored and anti-Government political meetings are banned. The ordinary citizen has no freedom to express himself in letters to a newspaper editor, except on "safe" subjects. By Western standards Islam has little freedom of expression but Mr. Mawdudi, whose thinking, his publishers say, has "influenced people all over the world," can claim it to be superior.

Through its spokesmen, such as Mawdudi, Islam is reacting to 100 to 200 years of Western domination.† Unfortunately, the political "attack" from the West was also seen as a direct attack on Islam as a religion. Professor Nasr says that the Muslim has "remained conscious of the fact that ever since his political subjugation his religion and his culture have been the target of innumerable assaults, ranging from out-and-out slander by older missionaries and Orientalists to much more subtle techniques of 'de-Islamicizing' the minds of Muslim youth in Western-owned and directed educational institutions in the Arab world."

To those of us in the West who know that there has been no such sinister perversion of the minds of Islamic youth Professor Nasr's outburst is sadly paranoid. But we

*Christian Science Monitor, March 3, 1980.
†"From Pakistan to Morocco the Muslim world is experiencing much the same phenomenon—a reaction against an over-hasty attempt to absorb the ideas of a different civilization." The Economist, February 17, 1979.

cannot dismiss it for it is a complex suffered by many Muslims. And it becomes the justification, among people less educated than Professor Nasr, for wanting to hit back at the West.

Professor Nasr's reasons for retaliating become clear when he writes of many Muslims displaying "a sense of inferiority vis-à-vis the West which is truly amazing." He also complains about "the paralyzing effect of modern Western thought upon the East and the Muslim world in particular." And he notes that "the West's impact on the Islamic world during the past century has brought havoc and confusion beyond comparison with anything that Islamic history has witnessed since its origin."

The confusion Nasr refers to can often be seen in the way Muslim world newspapers evaluate the West. For instance, in the press of Algeria, Tunisia and Morocco *Europe* is synonymous with *debauchery*.

Insisting that modern civilization as it has developed in the West since the Renaissance has failed, Professor Nasr believes that the teachings of Islam can help Western man to find a way out of the morass of modernism.

Altaf Gauhar presents an almost contrary point of view.* In his opinion the Islamic world is constantly providing the West with "evidence that Muslims do not seem to be fully conscious of the challenge and the requirements of modern times. Their answer to every crisis is to withdraw into the past. If you are committed to a backward-looking stance how can you keep pace with those who are forward-looking?"

Criticism also comes from Muslim scholars trained in the West to question, analyze and criticize. They blame the traditional élitist classes of Islam for introducing the regulatory and punitive parts of the Islamic system without doing anything to improve the social and economic order of the common people.

While Islam demonstrates its strength in Iran and Pakistan, the faith fights to keep its hold on Muslims in the United States and other Western countries. In 1980 the State Department estimated that perhaps four million

*Guardian Weekly, February 25, 1979.

foreign-born Muslims live permanently in the U.S. In addition the U.S. is a temporary home to about 300,000 Muslim students at any one time; at least 50,000 Iranians were studying at U.S. universities and colleges at the time of the seizure of the American embassy in Teheran. Another 300,000 Iranians are permanently resident in the U.S., mostly in Philadelphia and Los Angeles.

Leaders of the Muslim community in the U.S., who go to some trouble to avoid personal publicity, reject the idea of complete integration in the country of their adoption. In this they are at one with Muslim leaders in Britain and France, two other Western countries with large Muslim populations. American foreign-born Muslim men are particularly disturbed about the liking of their women for American freedoms—the ordinary right to dress as they like, to keep whatever company they choose and to work outside the home. Muslim men born in America are less strict about traditional taboos but they too worry about the "corrupting influences" of American life on their women. Such influences make them less dependent on the men and this is a blow to their male pride and against the security they have traditionally drawn from being in unquestioned control of the family.

It is known that many Muslim heads-of-family ban television in their homes for fear that such programs as "Charlie's Angels," "Police Woman" and "Wonder Woman," among others, will somehow pervert their daughters.

The Muslim resident community is no threat to the stability or security of the United States, if only because they are widely spread out; the largest community is 100,000 in metropolitan New York. In smaller Britain the one million resident Muslims are heavily concentrated in London, Bradford and Sheffield and constitute almost a nation within a nation. The establishment of the Islamic Council of Europe in London in 1973 was a significant step since it constitutes a base for the dissemination of Islamic information and influence. In the U.S. this is the function of Islamic foundations or centers in New York, Los Angeles, Detroit, Washington D.C., Cleveland and

North Caldwell, New Jersey. An important activity of the principal center in Washington is "to welcome and assist converts to the faith of Islam." In 1980 the center expected that about 100,000 Americans of various denominations would become Muslims.

The directors of Islamic centers, whether in the U.S. or in Europe, say that no resurgence of Islam is taking place, merely a reassertion. The uniformity of their statements suggests that they are presenting a prepared attitude. They say that what is happening is not so much a triumph over Christianity as an assertion of Islam, a religious and moral view of life, against the secular modern society of the West. The use of the word *against* is characteristic of Muslims describing the relationship between Islam and the West. An aggressive word, it explains Islam's reaction to its conviction that the West has been against Muslims. That there are still tremendous differences between the Muslim world and the West is obvious and natural. What is less obvious but more serious is that the tradition-minded rulers of Iran, Libya, Saudi Arabia, Pakistan and other countries are bent on emphasizing the differences rather than diminishing them.

The extremism of some American Black Muslims approaches the fanaticism of Iranian or Iraqi fundamentalist groups at its worst. The Black Muslim cult, which uses the Koran or a certain perversion of it, preaches a fanatical hatred of whites based less on actual injustice than on a mystic prediction of black world dominance. In 1973–74 twenty-three white San Franciscans were murdered or maimed by Black Muslim extremists, all young men, impressionable and prone to violence.

They have little in common with foreign Muslim students, who stay in the U.S. for two to five years, mainly to soak up technology which they can take back to their own countries in the form of job-capital. An American or European degree gives them an advantage over their contemporaries educated at home. The great majority indulge themselves in every comfort and convenience which the West can offer—including sexual liberalism—but on return to their own countries they condemn

"American perversions." Their own people expect such condemnation but it exasperates their American hosts.

Equally exasperating is the attitude of some Muslim academics resident in the United States. While resisting integration into American society, they attack Western scholars and writers for perpetuating divisions between Oriental and Western cultures. Professor Edward Said, a Palestinian who is Parr Professor of English and Comparative Literature at Columbia University, unwittingly illustrated a common Muslim defensive-aggressiveness towards the West in an article in *Time* Magazine.* Professor Said writes: ". . . One of the strangest, least examined and most persistent of human habits is the absolute division made between East and West, Orient and Occident. . . . Nobody bothered to judge Muslims in political, social, anthropological terms that were vital and nuanced rather than crude and provocative. . . ."

The trouble could be that Muslims themselves have not made their own political, social and anthropological terms clear enough. The "absolute division" which Said refers to has been extensively examined by Western students; Said himself counts 60,000 books on Islam and the Orient between 1800 and 1950. It is difficult to believe that all 60,000 lacked vitality and nuance; in any case, having complained that nobody is kind to Islam, Said approvingly quotes a Western Orientalist scholar, Louis Massingnon, who sympathetically called Islamic life "a science of compassion, knowledge without domination, common sense not mythology."

Certainly some Westerners are as sweepingly critical of Islam as Professor Said and others are of the West. Many politicians want to induce the Muslim world to accept modernism without reservation or equivocation. They do not know Islam. The proposition is unacceptable to Muslims because it ignores their innate sense of destiny. The Arabs particularly see the West as a cultural upstart, and to have to learn from it is a great dishonor.

The West is not overtly challenging Islam at all, but the Islamic states feel themselves under attack, and most

---

*April 16, 1979; and in his book *Orientalism*, Pantheon, 1979.

seriously by Western culture, drugs, drink, pop music, pornography. To us in the West these might be merely the raw materials of a sub-culture but to Islamic zealots they symbolize the West and illustrate its decadence.

Western students of the Arab world have repeatedly remarked on the violent hate that Arab Muslims feel for the West. In the mid-1950s Wilfred Cantwell Smith of Princeton University wrote: "Most Westerners have simply no inkling of how deep and fierce is the hate, especially of the West, that has gripped the modernizing Arab." A few years later Bernard Lewis of the University of London, described the Arabs' "revulsion from the West, and the wish to spite and humiliate it." When President Nasser made his arms deal with the Soviet Union in 1955 the Muslim world was immensely satisfied, Lewis suggests, because this was a blow against the West. "In the twilight world of popular myths and images the West is the source of all evil—and the West is a single whole." Emotionally it is satisfying to hold the West culpable for all the disasters which befall the Muslims.

And there is little chance of Britain and the West developing much in common with Islam. The West is defensive and apologetic, Islam aggressive and confident; the Christian West has compromise built into its ethics, while Islam has built-in inflexibility.

Marvin Zonis, a specialist on Iran at the University of Chicago, observes that in Iran and elsewhere, "Islam is being used for striking back at the West, in the sense of a people trying to reclaim a very greatly damaged sense of self-esteem. They feel that for the past 150 years the West has totally overpowered them culturally and in the process their own institutions and way of life have become second-rate."*

*Time magazine, April 16, 1979.

11

ISLAM AND ECONOMICS

An inner tension which has afflicted Islam in modern times concerns its attitudes to economics. Two factors in particular have aggravated the tension: 1. The great wealth from oil for many Muslim countries since 1945. 2. The emotional need to be different from the West in economic principle and practice. But oil wealth makes it difficult for the Arab countries to be different because, inevitably, they are linked with the capitalist practice of their foreign customers.

The Koran, and Muslim tradition, look with favor on profit, trade and production. "Merchants are the messengers of this world and God's faithful trustees on earth," said the Prophet. Also, the Koran is not against capitalism; in fact, it has no views on it. It accepts private property, inequalities in possession and wage-labor.

Islam is hostile, though, to unrestrained market speculation, large amounts of money held by banks as capital, state loans, indirect taxes on goods of primary necessity, such as oil for cooking. There is, too, a total prohibition on any selling in which there is an element of uncertainty or risk. Theoretically this makes sales by auction impossible, since the seller does not know for certain what price he will get. Even so, in 1956 I saw Muslim traders running a slave auction in Djibouti and the prices were highly uncertain since they depended on that imprecise quality of "desirability." Since then Islamic specialists in

81

law have explained to me that the Traditions make an exception of slaves.

It might seem that Islamic economic rules are spiritual in basis—and indeed Islam's egalitarian concept is attractive, with the contribution everybody has to make, through the tithe, to the community's resources. But as a distinguished student of Middle Eastern economics has pointed out, "Not by the wildest stretch of the imagination could the commercial communities of any Middle Eastern city be labeled 'spiritually oriented' or as holdouts from the chase after Mammon. Indeed . . . they are every bit as demonic and as much believers in social Darwinism as American and British businessmen of an earlier era."*

The "demonic" nature of Islamic economics is best illustrated in the way Muslim businessmen and bankers, and ordinary people, face the difficulties imposed by the Islamic ban on usury. Lending money at interest is a serious offense but ways exist of getting around it without much risk. For instance, Islamic banks take an equity in the projects they finance, say 20 per cent of the profits. But equally they are liable to share any losses, so this safeguards them against lending money at interest. Banks in Islamic countries are even less inclined to take risks than those in the West. In any case they charge a fee for "service and commission."

The Muslim world has many moneylenders catering to the needs of the hard-pressed. Their interest rates are exorbitant but any *hila* (ruse to escape punishment) is enough to keep both partners in the transaction on the right side of the law. A common ruse, the *mohatra* contract, has been in use since the Middle Ages. It works like this: Assume that I am a moneylender and you have come to me for money. I say to you, "You ask me to lend you a thousand dollars but as we are Muslims I cannot make you a loan and charge you interest. But I have a fine camel which I will sell you for fifteen hundred dollars, payable in a year's time. Agreed? Good. No, I have

*A. J. Meyer, *Middle East Capitalism*, 1960.

changed my mind—I will buy the camel back from you for one thousand dollars. Here is the cash."

I still have my camel, you have the money you want and in twelve months you will pay me $1500—the loan plus 50 per cent interest. The subterfuge is crude but it seems to be accepted by the authorities.

Maxime Rodinson quotes a case in Fez, Morocco, where certain Muslim merchants lent money at high interest. A particular wealthy merchant was approached by a co-religionist who needed a loan. The merchant sent out for some sugar which he then sold the would-be borrower at an enormous profit; the transaction went into the accounts book simply as money owing for sugar—at a rate of 400 per cent interest. A deed was drawn up with a house belonging to the borrower as security. At the end of the loan period, three months, the borrower could not pay for "the sugar." He was allowed further time, with the interest being doubled, and he soon lost his house. "All this was accompanied by the moneylender's pious moral formulas about the service he was rendering and the mutual aid that is proper between Muslims", says Rodinson.

Usury can also be avoided, or evaded, by barter. I want to raise some money so you give me two bushels of wheat which I can sell. After an agreed period I return to you three bushels, the third one being an "outright gift." Your interest lies in the money you can get for the extra bushel. Provided we talk about "gifts" during our transaction the religious authorities will not intervene. It is possible to buy books listing the tricks by which usury may be safely practiced.

Whether the Islamic legalists like it or not, in some countries bank loans with interest are breaching the Islamic code. In Afghanistan, in 1948, many years before the Communist take-over, four credit houses existed primarily to make low-interest loans to small businesses, farmers, cottage industries, animal breeders and others.

Rodinson says that the precepts of Islam have not seriously hindered the capitalist orientation taken by the Muslim world during the last hundred years. Islamic entrepreneurs, particularly those from the oil states, want easy, quick and certain gains from their investments—this is in keeping with the old Islamic horror of risk. They dislike investments which tie up a lot of capital and are slow in yielding a return. They engage in many activities and enterprises, few of them specific in character. According to Rodinson they tend to want to do everything themselves, having little appreciation of the need for technical advice and the advantages to be gained by investing money in research. "Research" is too nebulous a concept. "They have the mentality of go-betweens rather than of leaders," Rodinson says.

Some Muslim writers have been at pains to show that nothing in their religious tradition is opposed to the adoption of modern and progressive economic methods. But while they have been so insisting, leaders such as General Zia in Pakistan, Colonel Gaddafi in Libya and Ayatollah Khomeini in Iran have demonstrated the precise opposite. They have clearly stated that Islam opposes many Western and democratic economic methods.

Some Muslim economists, sponsored by political leaders with reforming zeal, have proposed an ideal Islamic economic system which would be based on private property, regardless of class. It would reject capitalist institutions such as interest while still operating productively. In Pakistan the Jamaat Movement proposes a personal income tax (zakat) of 2½ per cent. The Movement would drastically restrict the right to own private property and would nationalize practically all the means of production and distribution.

A good many naive suggestions are made. The Iraqi government official, M. F. Jamali says: "Wealth must not be hoarded and treasured; it must be circulated from hand to hand." This, he claims, is a principle of a sound Islamic society. Whatever the principle, enormous wealth *is* being hoarded and treasured. Armed with oil and petro-dollars the Arabs' economic influence is immense and stretches far beyond the traditional areas of Arab, Turkish and Persian domination. Usury might be forbidden, but the oil sheikh's capital is earning interest at a staggering rate. Those reformers within Islam who want a return to the fundamental and to the purity of ancient Islam are silent when it comes to the massive profits made from the investment of oil money in Western capitalist enterprises. Not that this is strange; making money out of infidels is hardly equivalent to the crime of exploiting fellow Muslims.

Libya, vastly wealthy from oil, has announced its own plans for a sound and equitable economy—"the third way" as President Gaddafi calls it to distinguish it from capitalism and communism. The government announced, in March 1979, that wealth would be distributed among the people, that houses are to be owned by those who live in them, land belongs to nobody and employees are now partners in the establishments they work in. Despite the notion about wealth distribution, Gaddafi had earlier announced that a man should not earn more than enough to cover his needs, defined as one house for one family, one car for one family and adequate food and clothing. Former owners and directors of businesses are now employees in their own companies, which are run by committees. All incentive to excel has been removed and mediocrity is cultivated. Cushioned by oil money, the Libyan economy will no doubt survive for a long time all that Gaddafi's "third way" can do to it.

I have heard many Western people, particularly politicians, accuse the Arab Muslims of ingratitude, on the grounds that it was Western vigor, technology and capital which found and developed the Middle Eastern oil fields and thus made the Arab states wealthy. That oil is a legacy of the colonialists does not make the Arabs any less liable to anti-colonialist slogans. The Western claim is irrelevant and as far as Islam is concerned a typical example of Western blasphemy and falsehood. We did not give them the oil—Allah did; we did not make the Arabs rich; Allah did that too.

12

ISLAM JUDGED BY ITS MINORITIES

Any country or society can legitimately be judged by the way in which it treats its minority groups.* Because they are potentially vulnerable in every way—physically, politically, economically, religiously—their status reflects the degree of tolerance or oppression of the ruling majority. There are, of course, ruling minorities, as in the Republic of South Africa, in which case there is inevitably armed repression of the majority. The Muslim world has no ruling minority, though it is possible that in some places a minority Islamic sect might have more power than a numerically larger one. At one time Lebanon had roughly even numbers of Christians and Muslims and this balance was reflected in parliament. So many Christians fled or were murdered during the civil war of 1975–6 that Muslims are in the majority but there is no effective government.

Basically, the minorities in the Muslim lands are Christians or Jews, with a considerable number of Hindus in Pakistan and a sprinkling of other peoples in several Muslim countries, notably Indonesia.

Officially, Islam tolerates minorities but a good deal of the Koran refers to the need or duty to kill unbelievers so

*And by the rights accorded its women; see next chapter.

at best the minorities are viewed with suspicion and incipient hostility by most Muslims. André Poutard, a prominent French journalist, wrote a long, considered article for *L'Express* (December 30, 1978) in which he noted that since the seventh century the history of Christians in the Koran-law countries had been nothing but a series of calamities and respites or "persecutions followed by periods of calm."

A scholarly researcher into Christians living in the Arab East, Dr. Robert Betts of the Johns Hopkins School of International Studies, says that as early as the eighth century the Christian communities and their leaders realized that the official Muslim toleration was "a prison from which there was no escape other than apostasy or flight."*

Islam established the *dhimma* (protected people) system for minorities. Originally the *dhimma* was the treaty concluded between Muhammad and those he subdued. They were tolerant pacts and in theory the *dhimmis* were guaranteed their lives and property, as well as their religious liberty, provided they did not transgress any of the *dhimma's* stipulations. But soon the *dhimma* became a codified system of legal tyranny. The Pact of 'Umar, generally attributed to 'Umar II (717–740) defined the status of the *dhimmis*. They had to pay the *jizya* (poll tax) symbolizing their subjection to Islam, and also higher commercial taxes than were paid by Muslims. Ownership of their land passed to the Muslim community and to have the right to cultivate it they had to pay another tax. The construction of new churches or the restoration of old ones, as well as the use of religious objects, such as the cross, was forbidden. *Dhimmis* had to live in separate areas in inferior homes. Marriage or sexual intercourse with a Muslim woman and blasphemy against Islam were punishable by death. Any relationship between Muslims and *dhimmis* was strongly discouraged, *dhimmis* were not allowed to testify in court against a Muslim and could exercise no authority over a Muslim.

*Christians in the Arab East, published by John Knox Press, Atlanta, 1975.

Dhimmis had to go unarmed, at great risk to their lives, while numerous decrees regulated the color and shape of their clothes, insisting on ill-fitting and ridiculous headwear, belts and shoes. Easily recognized, they were then humiliated in the street. A little bell around the neck or some other distinctive sign made them recognizable in the public baths. Horses and camels were reserved for Muslims, the *dhimmis* being allowed only to ride donkeys. In some periods Christians were forced to ride their donkeys facing the tail.

Dhimmis were supposed to do nothing to disturb Muslims, so they had to hold their church services in silence and they could not make public lamentation at funerals—a custom of the East. They had to stand up and remain standing in the presence of Muslims, address them humbly and give them right of way on the footpath, which meant walking on their left side—the impure side for a Muslim. The poll tax was paid at a ceremony during which the *dhimmi* was given a slap on the face or a blow on the neck as a sign of his inferior status.

All this was particularly galling to the Coptic Christians, who were the descendants of the early Egyptian Christians. Before the Arab invasion, Egypt had been a province of the Byzantine Empire; Egypt's inhabitants were primarily Christians and the land had many churches and monasteries. As they considered themselves the "original Egyptians" the Copts were distressed to be relegated to second-class citizenship in their own land.

Nevertheless, by the seventeenth century Christians were seriously revising their long tradition of learning and its high standards under the instruction and influence of Catholics and later Protestant missionaries. In contrast, education for most Muslims consisted of rote memorization of the Koran, and then only for men.

The persecution drove the Christians back into the strength of the family unit, and into reliance on the Christian community. Largely because of the stabilizing influence of the family and the stronger role of the parents, young Christians in Islam are still rarely guilty of crime.

History is full of maltreatment of Christians and Jews down the centuries until the founder of modern Egypt, Muhammad Ali (1801-46) improved the lot of Christians. The Copts particularly made much progress and when the British occupied the country in 1882 they became the civil servants of the new regime. Unfortunately, in Muslim thinking this linked Eastern Christians to the West, with further Muslim hatred for the Copts.

Numerous nineteenth-century documents, as well as reports by European travelers, confirm that the discriminatory status applied to the Jews under Islam continued under one form or another in most Arab lands until the early years of the twentieth century. Thousands of Jews were murdered singly, and collectively, *as Jews,* in Islamic lands from the Atlantic to the Persian Gulf during the half century before World War I. Forced conversions were not infrequent, often after girls and youths had been abducted.*

Under European rule, Christians and Jews enjoyed physical security—and some even a certain affluence—which lasted for two or three generations. As each Arab country won its national independence, the situation of the minorities worsened, often becoming intolerable. More than one thousand Jews were killed in anti-Jewish rioting from 1938 to 1949 in Baghdad (1941/46/48). Tripoli (1945/48), Aden (1947), Aleppo (1945/47/48), and Damascus (1938/45/49), Oudja, Djerade, Cairo (1948). Similar tragedies happened during the same period to many indigenous Christian groups throughout the Muslim Arab world.

A few leading Copts tried to solve their dilemma by publicly declaring, "I am Christian by religion but Muslim by nationality." The tactic was not widely successful. An authority on the Copts in Egypt, Y. Masriya, says that while "it is possible to be a Muslim and not an Arab, the reverse is impossible; a true Arab must be a Muslim."

*D. G. Littman, *Jews Under Muslim Rule in the late 19th century,* Wiener Library Bulletin Nos. 35/36, London, 1975; *Jews Under Muslim Rule: Morocco 1903-1912,* WLB Nos. 37/38, London, 1976; Ibid.

The idea is hateful to the many Arab Christians who can lay claim to an Arab genealogy as pure as that of any sayyid or direct descendant of the Prophet Muhammad.*

President Nasser made much of Islam as an essential focus of Arab identity. He did so to further his own ambitions, to make Egypt leader of the Arab world, and to achieve a degree of unity in the Arab world produced by no other leader. He did all this at the expense of the religious minorities living within that world. The Nasser tactics were a dreadful example of the immorality of political expediency. By closely linking Muslim values and identity with Arab nationalist goals he made it impossible for many Christians to become full members of the Arab club. For centuries the Christians had seen themselves as the link between East and West; Nasser insisted that they commit themselves to the East and become, in political effect at least, Muslims.

That non-Muslims are still held to be inferior is shown by Antoine Fattal, in his authoritative study on their legal status:

> The dhimmi is a second-class citizen. If he is tolerated, it is for reasons of a spiritual nature, since there is always the hope that he might be converted; or of a material nature, since he bears almost the whole tax burden. He has his place in society, but he is constantly reminded of his inferiority ... In no way is the dhimmi the equal of the Muslim. He is marked out for social inequality and belongs to a despised caste; unequal in regard to individual rights; unequal as regards taxes; unequal in the Law Courts. No fellowship is possible between Muslims and dhimmis ... Even today, the study of the jihad is part of the curriculum of all the Islamic institutes. Students are still taught that the holy war is a binding prescriptive decree, pronounced against the

*In 1979 the Egyptian Government quoted the Coptic proportion of the population at 7 per cent (of 39 million). This is as suspect as the Copts' own figure of 15 per cent. The real figure is probably about 10 per cent, or 3½ million in 1979.

Infidels, which will only be revoked with the end of the world.*

André Pautard asks "Whether the convulsions that constantly grip the Middle East are not in reality episodes of a religious war that has been going on for thirteen centuries—despite declarations to the contrary."

A Muslim historian told Pautard, "My real frontier is that of my faith." Charles Helou, a former Christian president of Lebanon, expressed himself more lyrically: "What is at stake here is less the land than each man's share in eternity, his right to paradise."

Since Christians and Muslims of much of the Orient both speak Arabic as their mother tongue they use the same word for God—Allah—and they frequently chant it in the same way. Pautard says: "The same word, the same chant, for two terrible divinities which are mutually exclusive. The one which Islam reveres considers itself perfect. Its message [the Koran]... is the ultimate expression of a divine message; this is unshakeable dogma. In Muslim eyes it reduces their Christian neighbors and compatriots to the rank of imperfect unbelievers, even of infidels, to the status of inferior citizens and, above all, to citizens of a society made for Muslims only, since the Koran scrupulously fixes all the religious, civil, social and personal ties of that society. 'You,' it says of the Muslims, 'are the best nation.'"

In this "best nation" the plight of the Jews reached sad proportions between 1948 and 1972 when most were driven out to become refugees. More than 260,000 left Morocco, 14,000 Algeria, 35,600 Libya, 30,000 Egypt, 130,000 Iraq, 50,550 Yemen, 4,500 Syria, 6,000 Lebanon and 108,000 left Tunisia.

President Sadat showed something of Muslim leaders' attitude towards minorities in a speech he made on April 25, 1972, celebrating the Prophet's birthday. I quote only briefly: "We believe, as commanded by Allah, that we are

*Antoine Fattal, *Le Stat Légal des Musulmans en Pays d'Islam*, Imprimerie Catholique, Beiruit, 1958 in Y. Masriya, *Les Fuifs en Egypte*, Genève, 1971.

a nation elected above all nations ... The Koran said of
the Jews, 'It was written of them that they shall be
demeaned and made wretched ...' and the Koran also
said of them, 'They shall be condemned to humiliation
and misery.' We shall send them back to their former
status ... Allah has made us the standard-bearers of the
most sublime of missions."

The 4,000 Jews remaining in Syria have certainly been
condemned to humiliation and misery. Their families
have been residents of Syria, mostly Damascus, for many
generations but they are used by the Syrians as possible
future "hostages" against Israel and as scapegoats when it
is necessary to find somebody to blame for an internal
crisis. During 1979, in the wake of Arab hostility to the
Israel-Egypt peace, they were deprived of the last vestiges
of freedom. They live in ghettos under curfew and a Jew
wanting to leave his neighborhood must report to the local
police station for a travel permit; if granted he must take
it to the police at his destination. No Jew may sell
property, in case he uses the cash to bribe his way out of
Syria. Jews may not bequeath anything to members of
their family and all property is confiscated on the owner's
death. The few Jews at universities owe their place to
bribes, and Jewish schools must be wholly staffed by
Muslims—an offensive stipulation. No contact is permitted with family abroad and all who have been in touch
with overseas visitors are interrogated and sometimes
tortured.

Syrian Christians are better off than Jews but under
oppression and discrimination their communities have
been shrinking steadily by emigration. For instance, the
city of Aleppo has 150,000 Christians but, as any one of
its six bishops will tell a visitor sadly, there should be
450,000. History offers them no comfort; in the first
centuries of the Christian era the Arabian peninsula had
fifteen Christian tribes. Nothing but archaeological curios-
ities remain of them.

In several countries distinctly Arabic programs of study
have been imposed on church schools and the rights of
Christian clergymen have been restricted. In Libya such
rights are non-existent; Gaddafi closed down all churches

in Libya in 1971. I have visited several where the altar has become a counter for selling drinks.

Few Western Christians appear able to conceive the altogether different role that their co-religionists must play in the life of the Middle East, where they are in proportion less numerous than racial minorities in the United States. Egypt's Coptic Christians, for instance, are frequently the subject of abuse, defamation and false report. As a correspondent of the *Christian Science Monitor* has reported from Cairo,* much inflammatory literature circulates from the Muslim University area. It purports to be written by the Coptic Bishop and other leaders of the Coptic faith and concerns "attempts to convert Muslims to Christianity." Other counterfeit leaflets attack the Islamic faith and call for the return of power to the Copts of Egypt.

Fundamentalist groups abhor the growing alliance between the U.S. and Egypt; they have convinced themselves that the Americans want to destroy them for the sake of Christians in the country.

In Iran leaders of the minorities have been worried since the Revolution and particularly since the writings of Ruhollah Khomeini have been made public. In one significant passage Khomeini wrote, "In Teheran, Christians, Zionist and Bahai missionary centers issue their publications in order to mislead people and to alienate them from the teachings and principles of religion. Is it not our duty to demolish these centers?"

Violent action nearly always follows inflammatory speech in Muslim countries. The leaders of *dhimmi* groups expect a bleak future, in which not the least of their worries is the apparent Western ignorance and disregard of their predicament.

*Phil Finnegan, March 17, 1980.

13

ISLAM JUDGED BY ITS WOMEN

To prepare for the celebration of International Women's Day in 1967 the Algerian newspaper *El Moujahid* in February and March opened its columns to its readers' letters on the topic. Many were too obscene to be published, others were perverted, hostile and narrow.

One male reader wrote:

> Allow me to say that the Algerian women's participation in the evolution of the nation is a catastrophe for the Muslim religion and a betrayal of the Koran. Allow me to say that the debauchery and the confusions in the present administration are due to women. It would have been better had they remained sequestered.

And another:

> Our socialism rests on the pillars of Islam not on the emancipation of the woman with her makeup, her coiffure, her finery, which causes unbridled passions to burst forth; the effect of these passions is detrimental to humanity as a whole causing discord and quarreling, the crimes which generally are

94

caused by women. I do not say that man himself is a saint but that he is confused and upset.

Yet this typical viewpoint was expressed in Algeria, where women had fought with men against French imperialism and in doing so had hoped that they would win equality for themselves, after centuries of repression by men.

The Koran itself is not unkind to women but it is patronizing, offering them protection along with orphans, imbeciles and other feeble-minded persons. It says nothing about their seclusion, except for the wives of Muhammad. One of the few Muslim men who has attempted to bring some rights to women, Qasim Amin (who died in 1908), insists that there is no general and strict order that women must cover their faces.

But one Koranic precept about women does have great influence. It is this extract from *Light* (Sura 24):

And tell the believing women to lower their gaze and be modest, and to display of their adornment only that which is apparent, and to draw their veils over their bosoms, and not to reveal their adornment save to their own husbands or fathers or husband's fathers or their sons or their husband's sons, or their brothers or their brothers' sons or sisters' sons, or their women, or their slaves, or male attendants who lack vigor (being castrated) or children who know naught of women's nakedness. And let them not stamp their feet so as to reveal what they hide of their adornment.

Under the special conditions applying in Mecca, women's faces are frequently unveiled in the mosque but their hair is covered with scrupulous care so that not a single strand escapes. They do this to avoid trouble from many fanatical men to whom "straying tresses are damnable coquetry," as the Dutch traveler Snouck Hurgronje puts it.

In practice women throughout the Muslim world have

been little more than possessions, secluded and veiled. In modern times their status varies from one country to another, as does their resistance to inferior status. In the Western world, which is largely ignorant about women under Islam, the two facts that everybody appears to know are that a man may have more than one wife and that divorce for a man is easy. In fact, he may take up to four wives, though he is advised not to have this many unless he can sexually cope with them. The Koranic injunction is: "If you fear that you will not deal equally then marry only one, or the female slaves." Islamic traditions strongly advise men to practice a rotation of sexual intercourse so that no wife is left feeling neglected.

Many Islamic scholars—and a good many lesser Muslims—say that pluralism in wives is more appropriate to the physiological nature of men, more compassionate towards women and more loyal to "liberties under God." The "compassion" is that some women would have neither protection nor sexual satisfaction if each man was limited to one wife. "Liberties under God" is a way of arguing that God has given men the *responsibility* of taking more than one wife.

The practices of veiling, seclusion and general social segregation of the sexes have helped to maintain two quite different societies in Islam—the world of men and the world of women. The two worlds have developed separately and much has yet to be learned about these separate worlds and the ways in which they interact without becoming integrated.

Whether in the beginning the seclusion of women then led men to find justification for seclusion or whether they were secluded as a result of male obsession with chastity is not fully clear. Certainly Muslim men have always put high value on female chastity before marriage. According to Mawlana Mawdudi, "The concept of sanctity of chastity and protection of women can be found nowhere else except in Islam."

This sweeping claim is absurd but under Islam loss of chastity is still viewed, in all classes and communities, as the gravest misbehavior. It is punished by the girl's father and brothers, the penalty varying from severe disgrace to banishment and even to death in some traditional communities. As for infidelity in a married woman, this is an affront not only to her husband but also, since marriage is a joining of families, to her own family. It is her father and brothers who administer the punishment, which, again, ranges from serious censure to isolation, banishment, or death. Not surprisingly, few Muslim women appear to have sexual intercourse before marriage.

The strict code forbids discussion of sex between men and women, even between husbands and wives, but it is a common topic among men and among women when the other sex is not present. Many village families live in one or two rooms, so children see and hear much of sex, but they must restrain the curiosity and interest which such familiarity arouses. Observers who have lived in villages report that children hear much sexual talk from the women especially. Winifred Blackman, a sociologist who spent some time in Upper Egypt, says, "Sexual matters form the chief topic of their conversation . . . Even before children adults discuss the most private matters without the slightest reserve, so that from their very early years children hear sexual matters spoken of and joked about."* But when they reach puberty boys and girls are placed under severe sexual restrictions.

Sexual relationships are dominated by male impulses and jealousy is one of the strongest. Kazem Daghestani says "The husband's jealousy derives from his pride and familial honor, rather than from love. His wife is his *'ird*, his honor. It is his honor which would be injured if his wife misbehaved."†

"Jealousy among us is a *tradition*," says Fadela M'rabet, probably Algeria's best known woman journalist.‡

Men are highly suspicious of women. They believe that women have strong sexual desires which they are too weak to control. They must then be carefully guarded; if they were not, they would soon disgrace their fathers and

---

*The Fellahin of Upper Egypt, Harrap, London, 1927. Little change has occurred in 50 years.
†Étude Sociologique sur la Famille en Syrie, Paris, 1932.
‡Les Algériennes, Paris, 1967.

brothers and husbands. Hence they are justifiably secluded and confined to their own company. One effective way of preventing misconduct has been child betrothal and marriage. A girl who is early promised to a man is under the surveillance of two families. Also, by selecting her husband when she is young, the family reduces the likelihood that she will be able to exercise her own judgment or preference, or even want to.

Morroe Berger believes that "Male suspicion of female sexuality is probably the counterpart of the great value men place upon their own sexual prowess. Though men boast of their virility, they must be careful not to become victims, through their wives and unmarried daughters and sisters, of the virility of other men."* The emphasis upon male potency is in line with early marriage, polygamy and easy divorce by the husband. In recent years, and especially in the cities and among the more educated classes, marriage occurs later, polygamy is fast fading and divorce is hedged about with restrictions which take women some way towards equality with men. But the consecration of male sexual vigor continues, and it increases unsatisfied male desires to the point where sex is an obsession with many young men. Dr. Sania Hamady, a Lebanese, says, "The code of sexual behavior is so strict and restraining that whenever an Arab man finds himself in solitude with a woman, he makes sexual approaches to her."† This may be an exaggeration but it indicates the extent of male preoccupation with sex.

In Fadela M'rabet's view many a Muslim in the grip of sexual obsession translates social progress into terms of debauchery and his mind invents women who fit his fantasy. "Thus, walking out freely by a woman becomes 'provoking,' a woman's pleasant smile an 'invitation,' and ease in attracting others becomes 'libertinism.' Not only Western women are then equated with whores but also all Algerian women who are a bit modern in their behavior."

By indulging in such fantasies, Miss M'rabet argues,

---

*The Arab World Today, Doubleday, 1964.
†Temperament and Character of the Arabs, Twayne, 1960.

men are freed from their obsession while keeping their consciences clear; then they feel *justified* in shutting up their sisters, while chasing their neighbors' sisters—since the neighbors' sisters are "bad girls."

Miss M'rabet, who had to leave Algeria for France to find a professional place for herself as a journalist and author, often writes with exasperation and frustration of Algeria's man/woman divided society. "In telling women what they ought not to do, not to wear, not to read, not to look at, and not to love, and by not explaining to them what they can become," she says, men are opposing themselves to all progress and continuing the confusion, hate, sectarianism and prejudice which already exist. "Such a passion for the past reveals a fear of the future, and this 'fidelity to the dead' is an affront to the living—and to the dead themselves."*

A Lebanese woman journalist, G'hadah al-Samman, also complains about men's attitudes. "In Arab society today, we find that the chastity belt is still forced on a woman, forced on her mind as much as or more than it is forced on her body. For a woman who allows herself to express freedom in her thinking and speaking will face strong public censure far more than does the prostitute who never bothers to face such a situation."†

The Koranic admonition to men to "protect" women is, like much else in the Koran, open to interpretation. The most gross manifestation of "protection" is the diabolical mutilation generally and euphemistically called "female circumcision." Islam is not to blame for introducing the various practices, but it is in Islam that they are mostly found in the twentieth century, as was established at a conference held in Khartoum in January 1979. The meeting, to find ways of countering the sexual mutilation of women and girls, was arranged by the World Health Organization in conjunction with the Sudanese Government. The 56 delegates who attended heard that at least 30 million women and girls, probably many millions more, have had their external genitalia removed, sewn up

*Les Algériennes, op. cit.
†In an interview published in Beirut in Mawaqif, 1970.

or infibulated—fastened with a clasp or buckle. The instruments used include razor blades, knives, fingernails, pieces of broken bottles, slivers of flint and the thorns of the dwarf acacia tree.

The "mildest" form of mutilation, the conference was told, consists of slicing off the tip of the clitoris with a sharp instrument, usually a razor blade. This practice is recommended by a number of Islamic authorities under the name "Sunna circumcision." It is at least less injurious than other types of mutilation. Franzesca Hosken of WHO believes that throughout 26 countries from Egypt to Nigeria, including the Yemens, Saudi Arabia, Iraq, and across to Jordan, Syria and southern Algeria at least 30 million women have had the whole of the clitoris as well as the inner lips excised by barbarous means.

The most radical form of mutilation is infibulation, which the Sudanese call "Pharaonic circumcision" and the Egyptians "Sudanese circumcision." It involves removal of the clitoris and the inner lips and then sewing up the labia majora whose inner surfaces have been previously scraped to ensure that they will stick together when they "heal." Apart from the great risk of infection or damage to other organs, the vast majority of the abused women become frigid.

The WHO delegates were told that the practice is standard in Somalia, Djibouti, Sudan, Upper Egypt, northern Kenya, Nigeria and many areas of Mali—that is, in predominantly Muslim countries.*

The Koran contains no reference to excision or infibulation. There is only a hadith, which says that the Prophet one day told Um Attiya, a matron who was excising a young girl, "Reduce but don't destroy." On this authority the authorities of al-Azhar encourage the "Sunna" form

---

*Details of the "operation" are not necessary here. They can be read in the WHO report, in Clair Brisset's account of the conference published in Le Monde and later in The Guardian (February 28 and March 1, 1979) and in Benoîte Groult's book Ainsi soit-elle (Grasset, Paris, 1975). Details of the ritual rape-in-marriage which follow the mutilations are also omitted here. They can be found in Jasques Lautier's La Cité Magique, Les Editions Favard, Paris, 1972.

of circumcision, which is said not to damage the woman. It is legal in Egypt and Sudan.

The basic reason for all these practices is again that men consider that women have a hypersexual nature which must be controlled—and in many places they have convinced the women of this, so that many girls ask to be excised; they believe that no man would otherwise marry them. Men are also supposed to obtain more pleasure with excised or infibulated women, an idea which has no basis in medical fact.

Pressure from women may eventually produce a climate of change but direct reform must come from men, since they are in control. A few male reformers exist, including Abdel al-Mar'a, who has written: "Man has stripped woman of her human attributes and has confined her to one office only, which is that he should enjoy her body. . . . Man is an oppressor in his home." He urged Muslims to look at the European countries "where the status of women has been raised to a high degree of respect and freedom of thought and action."

One of the few Arab Muslim leaders to accord women a place in public life is Colonel Gaddafi who considers the Libyan woman a co-revolutionary and many young women work in government offices. I have been interviewed and photographed by Libyan presswomen and I have dined out in a restaurant not only with men but with their wives as well; this could not happen in many Muslim countries. Perhaps in time the influence of the Islamic non-Arab world will be felt in the Arab countries. In Pakistan, Malaysia and Indonesia women have been much more free for a long time, though in Pakistan the Jamaat Party opposes the idea of women going out to work.

It would be a mistake to think that all women in Islam hunger for the feminist ideals of the West. Many have no conception of these ideals, others are frightened by them, some detest them. Yet others, having enjoyed a degree of freedom for a time, are reverting to old customs. Egyptian women have not been veiled for decades but in the late 1970s a new costume began to appear in Cairo and Alexandria and even in country towns. It is an enveloping neck-to-ankle robe, sometimes accompanied by a cloth mask with two eye-slits. The young women who have taken to this outfit also wear gloves and cover their heads. Mostly from non-Orthodox homes, these young women will tell you that they have adopted this form of dress to "defend Islam." I asked one girl "To defend it against what?" Her reply: "Well, perhaps defend is the wrong word; to serve Islam." But "defend" is not the wrong word at al-Azhar. In 1977 its governing council decreed that women and girls entering its doors must have their heads and faces covered, and it has endorsed the new style.

In Tunisia, the most Westernized of France's former North African colonies, women university students have reverted, though under pressure, to traditionally "modest" forms of dress.

Iran provides the most significantly topical study. During the Shah's regime the general picture was one of increasing freedom and equality for women, but it was not appreciated in the West that these freedoms were given grudgingly, and that few men believed in their propriety. Even Professor Seyyed Nasr, educated in the West and resident there for many years, wrote in 1975, "To accept one's destiny as a wife and mother ... of necessity concerned with daily problems, and to submit oneself to one's duties, have led many Muslim women to an intensely contemplative inner life amidst the type of active life imposed upon her by the hands of destiny." He is expressing the belief, held by most Muslims, that a woman's greatest purpose is to provide her husband with a son.*

Despite the progress made by women with the Shah's blessing, 53 per cent of Iranian women remained illiterate in 1979 and for them the only means of survival is marriage and their only protection the family. That the

---

*In Iran, as elsewhere in Islam, it has long been said that a man should have sexual intercourse with "a woman for a son, with a goat for relief and with a boy for pleasure." This was not to deny the pleasures of union with a woman but, mutilated as she so often was, she could not provide the satisfaction of a young boy.

progress of the others was not made with the blessing of Islam was shown by the Ayatollah Khomeini who at a stroke reversed most of the rights women had won and ordered them back to the restrictions and repressions of the past.

Even during the spectacular demonstrations, when one would have expected to find a pervasive equality, the women in their black veils (chador) were always in groups apart and were often herded along like cattle by the young men acting as marshals.

Many Iranian women, confused by change, were glad to hide themselves under the security of the chador as the Revolution arrived. Those who had actually fought for the revolution welcomed Khomeini's orders. After all, they wanted a return to the virtues of Islam, which they saw as liberation rather than restriction. But the women's considerable good-will to Khomeini quickly weakened when he went too far in his attempts to put women in their traditional place. The younger women, for instance, did not mind dressing in the chador—which at least protected them from odious ogling by men—but they did not expect to lose their livelihood as secretaries. The ayatollah banned women as secretaries, he said, because "Iranian secretaries have traditionally been sex objects."

The novelty of the Khomeini revolution wore off in a matter of days for the bright and educated Iranian girls. Tennis clubs were told to ban mixed doubles and women were required to wear slacks and long-sleeved shirts rather than the standard fashionable outfits. More seriously, changes were made to the Family Protection Law which had given women equality in divorce and family property. Under the changes women are at the mercy of their husbands.

On one memorable day in March 1979 several thousand chanting women marched through driving snow from Teheran University to the Prime Minister's office building, where they vainly tried to see Bazargan to protest about the withdrawal of their rights. Another group marched to the home of Ayatollah Taleghani, the second most important religious leader, where they handed in a petition. Under pressure, Khomeini relented enough to say that there was nothing wrong with women working in government ministries but they should be clothed according to religious standards and not appear "naked at work." He was referring to women wearing Western dresses and nylons.

Several women protesting in the streets were badly hurt by men acting under the orders of religious leaders to break up the gatherings. Some were stabbed and others clubbed.

Watching the hard-won freedoms disappearing one by one and the old male domination returning, Mrs. Jaleh Shambayati, a Teheran lawyer, made a bitter comment to an American journalist, "Islam gave women life 1,400 years ago, but the right only to breathe is not enough today."*

On May 17, 1979 to celebrate the birthday of Fatima, daughter of the Prophet Muhammad, 100,000 chador-clad women were organized to march through Teheran in a display of Muslim fervor. Converging on Teheran University they heard religious leaders congratulate them on their "contribution to the Islamic revolution." Kohmeini told them, "If Fatima had been a man she could have become a prophet as great as Muhammad." The women apparently saw nothing patronizingly sexist in this statement. But a girl student in jeans and blouse told a *Daily Telegraph* reporter,† "These women think they're getting freedom. If only they realized that Islam for women means the Dark Ages."

Something of these "Dark Ages" is known to Western girls, mostly English and French, who have become nannies in the homes of wealthy Muslims. Joining a Muslim family in England or France, the Western girl finds her job satisfying and her employers courteous and correct. But dreams of opulent living in a minor palace in Saudi Arabia or elsewhere vanish almost on arrival there. Most girls find themselves virtually imprisoned, with the man or men of the house demanding sexual favors. Since a foreign employee cannot leave Saudi Arabia without an

---

*Jane O'Reilly, *Time* magazine, April 2, 1979.
†Tony Allen-Mills, May 18, 1979.

exit permit some girls have been driven to desperate measures in efforts to escape, including overdoses of drugs calculated to get them into hospital but not to kill.*

*For an account of English girls in Muslim employment abroad see *Woman's Own*, May 26, 1979.

14
A TASTE OF LITERATURE

Style and taste in literature, and reaction to literature, is yet another way in which Western people can understand Islam. In a short book which deals with many aspects of Islam it is only possible to give an outline and my selections are chosen for what they reveal of Muslim attitudes rather than for literary merit.

As many Western students of Arabic literature have noted, it contains much repetition and standardization. Professor Gibb explains this by his observation that the Muslims' "physical environment has molded their habits, thought and speech, impressing on them those repetitions and abrupt transitions which are reproduced in nearly all aspects of life and literature." A leading Arab literary critic, Elie Salem, has remarked of Islamic prose literature that "thought comes in flashes . . . not in an unfolding, exhaustive and full rational order." Even in books dealing with political history there is often little or no relationship between successive paragraphs.

Originality is not valued in Muslim literature, because all originality began and ended with Muhammad and what was recorded in the Koran and Hadith, both of which adjure Muslims against any further literary invention. Originality is therefore blasphemous. Muslim authors restate a well-established theme, often with further elaboration or embellishment. Frequently a writer will restate his own theme several times in a single work.

When reading Muslim prose I am constantly reminded of the Koranic advice not to become involved in what you do not know. Muslim authors obey this and do not step off the well-worn tracks. Their readers need to have their opinions reinforced, not to have their minds disturbed by new ideas.

Words are immensely important to the Muslim, for words are acts; what a Muslim says, *is*. A modern Arab writer, Darwish al-Jundi, has said: "The Arabic language is the strongest foundation of Arab nationalism. It has drawn together the [people] of various countries and has been the means of communication of mind and spirit since the emergence of Islam. . . . The Arabic language has displayed a tremendous vitality in its structure . . . and its flexibility, binding the past to the present and consolidating nationalism. The imperialists fought it and tried to replace it with their own languages . . . hoping to stamp out classical Arabic, tear the links between Arabs and weaken Arab sentiment, which is everywhere nourished by the language."*

Darwish's language is so extravagant and his accusations against the West—most of them specious—so full of rhetoric that it makes its own point about the strength of Arabic language within Islam.

Poetry was always a fundamental of Arab Muslim life and when a poet appeared in a family the neighboring tribes would gather together and wish the family joy. A poet was regarded as a defense to the honor of them all, a means of perpetuating their glorious deeds. Much Muslim poetry is vainglorious. The poet glorifies himself and his family and his tribe. The traditional poems are full of menaces and challenges and obscenity is commonplace. A constant theme is blood-revenge, with poems explaining the poet's courage and resolution and contempt of death. They also reveal extreme cruelty and ferocity and the poet, or his subject, exults over the corpses of the men he has slain.

Even the more modern poetry, evocative though some

*In an essay in *Political and Social Thought in the Contemporary Middle East*, Prager, 1968.

of it is, rarely touches abstracts, almost as if ideas are too nebulous to be comprehended, too fragile to be handled. Nevertheless, much sensitive modern poetry is being written, a good deal of it sad in tone. Here is a particularly telling poem-song:

AND MY MOTHER BEGAN TO CRY

When he came in with my mother
And sat down in the shade,
I knew what his coming meant.
But so what? Many others besides me,
Many others have been divorced!
The men say, "Women are bad."
And the women say there are hardly any good husbands.
Mine was so naïve, he let himself be plucked
Like a young partridge from the nest.
That other, she knew how to seduce him and I'm sorry for him,
But also for myself, for I bear his child,
A child he doesn't care much about,
He talked and talked—what good are his fine words
When I feel like swords are plunging in my womb,
And sharp knives are cutting at my heart?
Well, I fought my two sicknesses,
The one in my heart and the one in my body.
I swallowed my grief, all my grief,
I didn't have to swallow my tears,
For I pressed my lips together tight before they fell,
I pasted a wide, a very wide smile
Across my weary and some would say dishonored face,
And that smile, which made me ill, told him
Of my contempt, but also my forgiveness and my pity.
He left, hardly turning his head,
And my mother began to cry.*

*Recorded from an oral recital by Mririda N'ait Attik in the Tachelhait dialect of Morocco by Rene Euloge in *Les Chants de la Tassaout,* Casablanca, 1972. Translated by Elizabeth Warnock Fernea in *Middle Eastern Muslim Women Speak,* University of Texas Press, 1977.

Some of the best of modern poetry came from the pen of an Iranian girl, Furugh Farrukhzed, who was killed in a road accident in 1967, when she was only 31.

THE HIDDEN DREAM*

O, hey, man who has burned
My lips with the sparkling flames of kisses,
Have you seen anything in the depth of
My two silent eyes of the secret of this madness?

Do you have any idea that, in my heart, I
Hid a dream of your love?
Do you have any idea that of this hidden love
I had a raging fire on my soul?

They have said that that woman is a mad woman
Who gives kisses freely from her lips;
Yes, but kisses from your lips
Bestow life on my dead lips.

May the thought of reputation never be in my head,
This is I who seeks you for satisfaction in this
    day.
I crave a solitude and your embrace;
I crave a solitude and the lips of the cup.

An opportunity far from the eyes of others
To pour you a goblet from the wine of life,
A bed I want of red roses so that one night
I might give you intoxication.

Oh, hey, man who has burned my lips
With the flames of kisses,
This is a book without conclusion,
And you have read only a brief page from it.

Before Furugh no woman poet in Persian had ever composed love poems with men as the love object and after none can escape her influence. Many younger Iranians regard her as the outstanding champion for the current generation of liberated Iranians—perhaps because

*Middle Eastern Muslim Women Speak, op. cit.

she so movingly depicted their own moods and crises of loneliness, alienation, surrender, resignation and silence.

Since the Ayatollah Khomeini's revolution Miss Farrukhzed's work has been banned as "erotic" though people who understand literature say that sensitive restraint is the quality which most marks her work. In any case, most of her poems are not about "love"; her passion is simply the passion of the poet.

It is instructive to look at what happened to the work of the famous Egyptian writer Taha Hussein, a genuine thinker in the Western sense. Born in 1889, Hussein became blind as a boy but later married an equally intelligent wife who was able to act as his eyes. In 1926 he published a book on supposedly pre-Islamic poetry, daring to use the methods of modern critical scholarship. He concluded that it was doubtful if the poetry had, in fact, been written before Islam. His book was fiercely criticized and Hussein's motives, scholarship and religious principles were assailed. The angry traditionalists—that is, practically everybody—were angry because Hussein's book suggested a critical method which, if applied to Islamic religious texts, might cast doubt on their authenticity and because it struck at the traditional structure of Arabic learning. The disturbance was so great that the publishers withdrew the book.

When Hussein questioned in one of his books whether Abraham and Ishmael had ever been in Mecca he was dismissed from his university post. Many years were to pass before he was reinstated.

For much of his life Hussein risked unpopularity and consequent poverty by being critical of what he believed was hindering the development of his beloved country. Islam, he said, should not be in charge of general education, and schools should teach the concept of territorial nationalism rather than the old and narrow religious nationalism. He argued that Coptic Christianity should be well taught as a state responsibility. This suggestion was treated as heresy. When he became adviser to the Ministry of Education in 1942–4 he helped to found the University of Alexandria, became its first Rector, and was able to put some of his ideas into practice. But in 1949 he was still writing despairingly that "This country which was made for freedom is still enslaved by blinkered traditionalists."

The Lebanese woman novelist, Layla Ba'labakki, also had trouble from the blinkered traditionalists. A Shi'a from southern Lebanon, Miss Ba'labakki was charged with obscenity and "harming the public morality" in a short story published in 1964 when Miss Ba'labakki was 28. In a beautifully written, sensitive love story the chief of the Beirut vice squad found two passages which contravened clause 532 of the criminal law. Even before the case came to court the squad was sent around to confiscate all known copies of the book. The passages were:

He lay on his back, his hand went deep under the sheet, pulling my hand and putting it on his chest, and then his hand traveled over my stomach.

And:

He licked my ears, then my lips, and he roamed over me. He lay on top of me and whispered that he was in ecstasy and that I was fresh, soft, dangerous, and that he missed me a lot.

As it happened, Miss Ba'labakki was found innocent after a long and tortuous trial.

For me, the most interesting aspect of modern Islamic literature is the part played by Muslim women poets and novelists. Because they are inspired by discontent and protest their work is much more lively and sensitive than that of Muslim men. It might well be that women will release Muslims from the chains which forbid originality, creativity and innovation and thus enrich the quality of Islamic life.

15

KEY COUNTRIES

This chapter is devoted to the problems posed by militant religious orthodoxy in the main Islamic countries.

EGYPT   *Consorting with unbelievers*

Relatively few Western people understood the real nature of the step President Sadat took in November 1977 when he began his peace initiative by flying to Israel as the first move in complicated negotiations. Several important Western politicians appreciated the courageous nature of Sadat's mission and they understood the economic reasons which compelled the Egyptian president to make overtures to Israel but they were bewildered by the bitterness he aroused in the Arab world. The hostility reached its height after the signing of the treaty in March 1979, when most Arab states severed diplomatic relations with Egypt.

The sheer hatred of President Sadat was religious in nature. By agreeing to peace with Israel he was, in the eyes of other Muslim Arab leaders, guilty of a crime against Allah, against the Koran, the Shari'a and against every tenet of Islam. He was making peace with a country still regarded as an enemy by Muslims. Aggravating his crime, he was consorting with unbelievers—and the very worst unbelievers, according to the theologians of al-

Azhar. Other Arabs compare the separate Egyptian-Israeli peace treaty with what they regard as the two historic catastrophes in their modern history. The first was the Sykes-Picot Agreement of 1916. Under this secret pact Britain and France divided up the Arab world into polities which the Arabs see as unnatural. The second "catastrophe" was the creation, in 1948, of the state of Israel. The rhetorical invective of Islamic world leaders against Sadat and in the press, is vicious, sustained and prolific. Egypt is described as a pariah, an outcast, a leper . . . the list of terms of abuse would fill a book.

Long before his historic mission—which Sadat invited other Arab leaders to join—Egypt had faced crises brought about by Islamic militants. The most important extremist group is the Muslim Brotherhood, founded by Hassan al-Banna (1906–49), which tried to assassinate President Nasser in October 1954. Six Brethren were then executed and many others were imprisoned. Al-Banna preached that Western civilization created all the major ideological evils—capitalism, fascism and communism. The Brotherhood equates Islam inextricably with nationalism and some members tried to murder President Sadat when they realized that his revolution was socialist rather than Islamic.

During 1978 the Brotherhood, though still officially prohibited from organizing in Egypt, was tacitly allowed to reappear at universities, which it has thoroughly infiltrated by gaining control of the student organizations. It publishes an influential monthly magazine. Without a coherent political ideology and with no firm ties to leftist dissidents—which they would need to be strong in numbers—the Brotherhood is not believed to be a serious threat to the President. But it sounds threatening—"The Egyptian Government is damned because it denies the sovereignty of God," the Brotherhood proclaimed in a statement of October 1978.

Other even more fanatical groups are bent on murder and destruction in the name of Islamic purity. In 1976 the Takfeer Wal Hijra (Atonement and Migration) group led by "Prince" Shukri Mustafa murdered the elderly former Minister for Religious Affairs, Dr. Sheikh Zahaby, for criticizing fanaticism. Shukri Mustafa and four others were hanged.

President Sadat has warned extremist religious groups against "exploiting the youth, distorting the facts and harming the homeland under the guise of religion." He has hanged some offenders and has urged his ministers to work on ways of adapting Islamic codes to the country's national laws, but attempts to "adapt" Islam constitute heresy in the views of the fundamentalists. Sadat's efforts to avert extremism are partly successful but they also inflame opinion. In 1979 a fresh clandestine movement, the "New Muslims," threatened to disrupt Egyptian life until the nation is "reformed"—which means a reversion to orthodox Islam. Apart from such groups something like an alliance of Marxists and politically conscious orthodox Muslims is in its nascent stages in Egypt and will cause trouble.

The imams are increasing their influence. In their harangues in Egypt's mosques they are winning audiences by stressing a theme which rivets the attention of young men—they talk about sinful men who cheat their wives with mistresses instead of taking a second spouse. They say that not only is it lawful to have up to four wives, it is fair to all, since each wife knows exactly how much attention the man is paying to the others. "A mistress is not only deceitful, she is encouraged to be voluptuous," the imams say. "A wife is not voluptuous—she has no need to be."

Fired by the imams' preaching against immorality, groups of mostly young Islamic moral vigilantes roam Cairo each night, obliterating with black paint any advertisement which displays women's breasts or thighs, even when they are decorously covered. Fundamentalists are even demanding the segregation of the sexes in restaurants and cafeterias.

Sixty per cent of Egypt's population is under 21 and the vast majority of them, even in the cities, are well behaved and not interested in clashing with the authorities. Even the students have suspended the habit of demonstrating in the streets. Boys and young men are television and cinema addicts; Cairo has 80 cinemas and an annual audience of 30 million. With few exceptions young men do not indulge in sports and they show practically no spectator interest. Cairo and its suburbs have nine million inhabitants—but not one public swimming pool. Since the sexes are strictly segregated there are no Western-type amusements and leisure activities. Street prostitution has declined so sexual repression finds its outlet in homosexuality. Rape is practically non-existent; no figures exist for incest and family rape but both occur to a degree which Western society would find disagreeable.

But if sex is not socially disruptive unemployment is. Egypt has no worthwhile jobs for qualified people; the pay is abysmal—the equivalent of 38 dollars a month as a young accountant, solicitor or surveyor. Young Egyptians long to leave Egypt. They plead with all foreign visitors believed to have any "influence" to get them a visa. They will emigrate anywhere. I mentioned casually to some students that I had a son living in Australia and at once several asked if he could get them visas to live in Australia. Several hundred thousand Egyptians left the country in the period 1969–79—the government says a million.

Among those who remain the most disillusioned are young civil servants who, as university graduates and often as army veterans as well, begin working at no more than 45 dollars a month. An acute housing shortage forces them to postpone marriage for up to ten years, assuming that by then they will somehow have the 3,000 dollars required as a down payment on a new apartment.

Vast numbers of naïve Egyptians expect the good life to follow final peace with Israel. But corruption and inefficiency are so rife, food is so scarce, the population increase is so great and Egypt's debts so vast that prosperity is a generation away. The message from the Egyptian government to the people is that they should not expect prosperity and abundance soon; they are working for a better life for their children and grandchildren. This moral exhortation means little to the great mass of younger Egyptians who are not yet even married. They want prosperity very soon, and if the Islamic fundamentalists promise it to them they might not long remain docile under the more pedestrian policies of socialist nationalism.

The ulama has an historic interest in seeing that the Egypt-Israel peace treaty does not work. More committed to Islam than to Egypt as a state they have a fertile field in which to sow their seeds of unrest.

Since the beginning of the century Egypt has been thought of as one Muslim nation which has come to pragmatic terms with its religion, but this is not now the case because the religious leaders do not want to come to terms with the state. They know that Egypt's volatile population will be disappointed in their expectations and when that happens the imams will be ready to exploit the situation by blaming the West and Sadat's treason. They will be aided—even if they reject the aid—by militant undercover groups incited by Libyan, Iraqi, Syrian, Saudi and PLO agitators. Egypt is a powder keg waiting for an Islamic fuse to detonate it.

PAKISTAN   *"Islam is kind and just"*

Because the Muslims of the Indian sub-continent cherished their religion they formed Pakistan in 1947, under the arch-pragmatist Muhammad Ali Jinnah. Sometimes known as "the land of the pure," Pakistan was to be a refuge for middle-class Muslims who could not live under the more dynamic Hindus, who were greatly in the majority. Religion has an intense emotional significance to Pakistanis, 95 per cent of whom are Sunnis.

The creation of Pakistan was a novel experiment in statehood and it posed the question whether religion— Islam in this case—could provide a strong enough bond to overcome the stresses of a plural society whose complex cultural differences were compounded by economic disparities and geographical separation of East and West Pakistan by 1,000 miles of hostile Indian territory.

The question was soon answered. Islam was *not* powerful enough to hold the two parts of Pakistan together in any sort of harmony. This was because the only real basis of Muslim unity in the sub-continent had been hatred of the Hindus. With the Hindus now sealed off in India the ideological conflict faded away. Without the cohesive factor of hatred, East and West Pakistan began to seek separate roads of self-interest and the more aggressive West Pakistan began to dominate the prosperous and populous East. For its own survival East Pakistan resisted, but the discrimination practiced by the Punjab-dominated West Pakistan against the Bengalis of East Pakistan was powerful and pervasive, even to the point of questioning the Islamic piety of the province's 60 million Bengalis.

For instance, West Pakistani leaders said that as Bengali was also the language of Hindus living in the Indian state of Bengal it was a "Hindu language" and therefore anti-Muslim. The Prime Minister, Liaquat Ali Khan, stated, "Pakistan is a Muslim state and it must have as its lingua franca the language of the Muslim nation . . . Urdu." This obvious absurdity—if the Muslim nation has a lingua franca it is Arabic—further incensed the East Pakistan people.

In December 1971 they broke away to form the Republic of Bangladesh. In human terms this revolt was terribly expensive. Bangladesh leaders claim that the Pakistan army embarked on a campaign of genocide and that in nine months it killed two million people in an attempt to crush Bengali-Muslim nationalism. Another ten million people fled to temporary safety in India and the war destroyed the economies of Bangladesh, Pakistan and India. The principal authority on Bangladesh, Anthony Mascarenhas, says that this conflict "is easily the greatest human disaster in modern times."*

Islamization of Pakistan began under President Bhutto. A politician with modern ideas and well aware of contemporary political movements, Bhutto tried to introduce reforms and to correct some of the glaring social inequalities. Nevertheless, this Westernized leader was forced to introduce punishment for printers who produced

*Case Studies on Human Right and Fundamental Freedoms, vol. 5, published by the Foundation for the Study of Plural Societies, The Hague, 1976.

copies of the *Koran* with printing errors. Under the weight of the mullahs' attack that he was responsible for the immorality of the country, Bhutto panicked and banned alcohol, gambling and horse racing.

With religious leaders and the more conservative circles becoming agitated about Bhutto's thrusting style of government and reforms, the army wrested power from him in 1977. Direct power fell to General Muhammad Zia al-Huq, though the dominant force in the ruling group is the Jamaat-i-Islami (Islamic movement), whose leader is the influential Mawlana Mawdudi. Saudi Arabia is the movement's principal sponsor and financier. General Zia shrewdly recognizes the power of the mullahs and panders to them as the principal power base of his rule. But Saudi influence is profound. The Saudis advised the officials of Islamabad on drawing up the Islamic laws, they pay for Pakistan's large arms purchases and they employ many Pakistani technicians and workers in Saudi Arabia. Pakistan also has close links with the United Arab Emirates.

Until February 1979 justice in Pakistan was based on the system handed down from the British colonial period, which in the mind of the zealots was reason enough to make radical changes to it. Presenting the "new" Islamic code of law to local dignitaries and foreign diplomats in February, General Zia said that he was concerned about the poor image of Islam abroad. "Islam is understood as a religion which does nothing else than say a hand should be chopped off or a man should be stripped naked and whipped." He claimed that some of its exemplary punishments were not likely to be carried out frequently, such as the public stoning to death for adultery.

At this meeting, Zia nevertheless recited the entire catalogue of punishments, starting with the amputation of a hand or foot for stealing or mugging. "If one severed hand can bring us six months of peace then it is worthwhile," General Zia said. Whipping is ordained for a number of offenses including attempted robbery and prostitution, maliciously suggesting that somebody, living or dead, has had sexual intercourse without being married; and drinking. A Muslim who takes alcohol can get 80 lashes, laid on in public. Non-Muslim foreigners may drink only in their embassies, residences or hotel bedrooms—or risk three years in prison and 30 lashes.

"Islam is a progressive religion which teaches you to be kind and just," Zia said. "The hard punishments of hand amputation and flogging are exemplary punishments for the good of mankind. A little knock on the knuckles will do you a power of good."

General Zia's insistence that Islam is benign also rests on social reforms, including two religious taxes brought back from Islamic obscurity. They are the *zakat* and *ushr,* both self-assessed and voluntarily disbursed. Zakat is a 2½ per cent wealth tax and ushr is a 10 per cent tax on the produce of irrigated farm land. It has to be paid in money or in kind—wheat or rice—by every peasant farming land over a hectare in size. Together the two taxes are supposed to bring in $75 million a year to be spent on feeding the hungry and housing the homeless. Success of this laudable idea depends on how seriously the Muslims of Pakistan take their Islamic duties. Many Pakistanis living abroad say that the new laws are nothing but a charter for cheating. How is it possible, they say, in a country where corruption is widespread to install a system based on voluntary honesty?

Islamization also affects education. Schoolbooks have been revised to bring them into line with Koranic precepts. From 1980 Urdu replaces English in schools—though Urdu is not the national language of the Pathan, Sindhi and Baluchi minorities. Information Minister Mahmud Azam Farooqi instructed television producers that they must make programs which are "essentially educative." And all programs, including recreation, should conform to the "ideology of Pakistan"—a concept which none of the religious leaders has defined.

Even General Zia found that he is vulnerable to the anger of the mullahs. When he opened an art exhibition in Karachi in February 1979 the President commented off-handedly that the fine arts had flourished in Islam's days of glory. When reported, this observation was met with scores of stinging letters and press statements from every Muslim sect protesting that sculpture and paintings other than abstracts were expressly forbidden in the Koran. It demonstrated the rigidity of the religious men. When they pointed out to Zia that dancing is part of the culture of the Hindus—an "enemy" people—he banned that as well. Music, which also does not conform to the religious code, is prohibited. A major issue during February and March was whether the sight of a woman's navel would offend Muslim sensibilities and drive men further into "immorality." And this in a country facing poverty, overpopulation, corruption, disease, political dissent and the danger of fragmentation.

The frivolous nature of the row over navels contrasted with the world furor which followed the sentence of death passed on Mr. Bhutto and his sufferings in prison. Some time before the crisis Mawlana Mawdudi had written that "To arrest a man only on the basis of suspicion and to throw him into prison without proper court proceedings and without providing him with a reasonable opportunity to produce his defense is not permissible in Islam."* Perhaps he considered that Bhutto had indeed enjoyed proper court proceedings and a real chance to defend himself, though many Western jurists would not agree.

Apart from this, conspiracy to murder—the charge against Bhutto—is not a capital crime under the Shari'a. General Zia brought in changes to the law to make it such a crime in the Bhutto case. He also instituted a religious bench of the Lahore High Court to ensure that the appeal for mercy made on Bhutto's behalf would get an unsympathetic response. There was never the faintest likelihood that Zia would show executive clemency. Because there is no compromise in Islam as a religion there is no compromise on those occasions when the religion becomes politics. This is why the appeals by practically every leader in the world for clemency for Bhutto made no impression on Zia. Nor did Zia show any common humanity; he did not inform Mrs. or Miss Bhutto about the ex-president's imminent death and they were not allowed to attend his burial. By Western standards the whole affair was shabby and shameful. More than any other

---

*In his treatise, *Islamic Law*, Islamabad, 1956.

single incident in modern times, Zia's treatment of Bhutto shows the uncompromising and merciless nature of Islamic law.

SAUDI ARABIA   Reluctant leaders

As the guardian of most of the holiest places of Islam, Saudi Arabia is the key Muslim country. Owner of 30 per cent of the world's oil reserves and wealthy beyond calculation, it is Islam's principal financier, providing money for development in fifty or more countries. While not militarily powerful it exercises tremendous influence throughout the world. In little more than a decade geography, geology and history have propelled Saudi Arabia from provincialism to a central position on the world stage.

Much of the Islamic world looks to Saudi Arabia for political guidance but its feudal leaders, ignorant about foreign affairs and unskilled in world politics, are in no position to provide guidance. Despite their wealth they are desperately insecure, since they face dangers from Communist expansion, from the PLO which would like to force Saudi Arabia to be more actively militant against Egypt, Israel and "the West," and from the fundamentalist religious leaders outside the country who cannot tolerate monarchies and would like to see the Saudi dynasty collapse.

The "home" of Islam, Saudi Arabia naturally resists change but the oil industry brings profound changes, if only as a result of the influx of foreigners. Despite the continuing viability of its patriarchal system of government—there is no organized opposition—the sheer pace of change is fast exposing it as an archaism.

Many observers predict that Saudi Arabia will go the way of Iran, with religious zealots bringing down the monarchy and creating another Islamic republic. But no true parallel can be drawn between the two countries. Unlike the Shah, a remote and isolated figure, the huge Saudi ruling family, with its estimated 5,000 princes, has its roots in the lives of its people. Its members are married into the families of commoners all over the country. Saudi rulers take their obligations seriously and even the lowliest citizen can approach King Khaled or Crown Prince Fahd with a complaint at their daily council. Another important difference is that the Saudi rulers maintain close links with the country's religious leaders and see that they are "well looked after." Since the early nineteenth century the House of Saud has had strong bonds with the puritanical Wahhabi sect of Sunni Muslims who dominate the country's religious life. On major issues the princes seek the opinions of the ulama, whose power was demonstrated in 1978 when they successfully demanded the razing of an entire modern city that had been built for pilgrims near Mecca, at a reported cost of 20 million dollars. The ulama ordered it destroyed because it "desecrated" a holy place, and the government reluctantly agreed.

The royal family also endorses the ulama's strict Koranic law. Two Britons were arrested and deported after being found with a lone woman at a seaside picnic, even though no impropriety was suggested. The woman was "righteously punished," which probably means that she was flogged. In September 1978 three men were beheaded after being caught having sexual relations with a woman in a tent, though adultery was not at issue. With the Islamic law so rigorously enforced by the state it is unlikely that religious leaders would ever lead a movement against the royal house.

While Saudi Arabia covers an immense area—one fourth of the size of the United States—it has a population of only eight million, many of whom are desert dwellers who could never fit into a modern army. Saudi Arabia's power does not lie in its military potential—though it can buy whatever armaments it desires—but in the Islamic example it sets to the Muslim world and in the terrorism and propaganda it finances. Saudi Arabia does not itself engage in terrorism but it pays large sums of money to the PLO as a form of insurance against the possibility of the PLO's taking an unhealthy interest in Saudi Arabia. While friendly to the United States because they need American help against Communism, the Saudis nevertheless financially support anti-Western propaganda because they must be seen to give a lead in jihad.

The truly unprogressive nature of Saudi society is illustrated by the resistance of the Wahhabis to the introduction of the radio and telephone, and later of television. Only when King Faisal pointed out that they could be used to transmit the words of the Koran were they permitted. Closed-circuit television has certainly proved useful; it permits women students in the universities to be taught by men. No male teacher is allowed into the presence of girl students.

The "Hoda affair" of 1972 indicates the extreme narrowness of the male-dominated Saudi society. Hoda, a twelve-year-old schoolgirl, answering a magazine questionnaire for fun, said that she was "in love" with a popular singer. For this shocking statement she was accused by the Director of Feminine Education, Sheikh Ben Rachid, of "immodesty" and blacklisted at all schools in Saudi Arabia. Hoda had to change her name and town of origin—no easy deception—to continue her schooling. When, in 1977, she applied to enter university she persuaded a newspaper editor to publish an article denouncing Sheikh Ben Rachid's "obscurantism." He replied with abuse and had the offending editor jailed for a week. To keep the affair quiet another official saw to it that Hoda could enroll at the university under her own name but she knows that the dice of the future are loaded against her if she remains in Saudi Arabia.

The attitude of mind evident in the Hoda case is also apparent in external affairs, such as in the anger the Saudis directed against President Sadat for arranging a peace with Israel. But this must be seen against the recent history of Saudi Arabia and its relations with Egypt. Saudi Arabia had been part of the Ottoman empire and King Ibn Saud did not gain full control over the Arabian peninsula until the 1930s; even then he did not hold Yemen or the British-controlled areas along the coast from Aden to Kuwait. Having taken over the vast desert areas he recruited Bedouin warriors to impose the austere Wahhabi version of Islam on the conquered populations.

After World War II the Saudi treasury shared the oil revenues 50-50 with the American-owned Aramco; this brought vast sums into the treasury but Ibn Saud's decadent son, Saud ibn Abd al-Aziz, soon managed to overspend. He was persuaded, in 1964, to abdicate in favor of Faisal, under whom Saudi's share of the oil revenue reached a billion dollars. But the industry had to employ many Palestinians, Syrians and Egyptians, who detested the traditional monarchy and expected Islamic salvation from Gamal Nasser, enemy of the Saudis. The first clear confrontation between Nasser and the Saudis took the form of a proxy war in Yemen. The republican regime proclaimed there in 1962 soon obtained military aid from Egypt so King Faisal supported the royalist side with money and arms. This Saudi support never enabled the royalists to win a clear military victory, but the withdrawal of Nasser's badly mauled troops by 1967 amounted to a defeat for any Egyptian ambitions to turn republican Yemen into a springboard for a takeover of the Arabian peninsula. After Egypt's defeat by Israel in the 1967 war, better Saudi-Egyptian relations made it possible for Faisal to compensate Nasser for the loss of 200 million dollars annually in Suez Canal revenues.

Faisal was assassinated by one of his nephews in March 1975, leaving his successor, King Khaled, with the "Egyptian problem." It receded for a time after the war of 1973 when Egypt surprised the Israelis and to general Arab delight made some initial gains but it returned when Sadat made peace with the enemy. The pressure on King Khaled and Crown Prince Fahd to "punish" Sadat became strong, though ironically they too need and want a negotiated peace so that they can face real enemies without being distracted by looking in Israel's direction. The Saudi rulers resisted the pressure for a time but then the state-controlled Egyptian press, in an extraordinary outburst, accused the Saudis of policies which would bring about a Communist takeover of Arab oil and the Muslim holy places of Arabia. After this it was not too difficult for the Saudis to sever diplomatic and economic ties with Egypt. Even so, they said they would honor agreements already in force, such as paying 525 million dollars for Egypt's purchase of 50 jet fighters from the U.S.

Saudi Arabia's future is not as secure as its wealth appears to indicate. It has withdrawn its troops from the "peacekeeping" force in Lebanon, indicating that it does not want to accept invitations to be the "regional superpower." This, they feel, might invite even more direct Soviet-aided aggression. Thrown violently off their Islamic course, the Saudis are looking for somebody to blame. And like everybody else in the region they blame the United States.

IRAN   "A chilling message"

Of all Islamic states, Iran provides the most striking example of the use of the dagger of Islam in modern times. Indeed, Iran (the old Persia) came into being by force. In 1921, Reza Khan, a sergeant who had risen to command the Czarist-trained Cossack Brigade and distinguished himself by ousting a Soviet regime from northern Iran, seized power in Teheran. The mullahs, in 1924, were largely responsible for wringing a constitution from Reza in their desperate efforts to prevent Iran from following the "bad" example of Ataturk's Turkey, which had turned secular. These mullahs induced Reza to crown himself as monarch and in 1925 he proclaimed himself Shah, with the newly adopted family name of Pahlevi. For sixteen years he ruled the country with a heavy despotic hand, building railroads and hospitals and otherwise trying to modernize the country.

Iran proceeded to have a checkered and often violent history. After World War II there were many riots and assassinations and much political turmoil, inspired either by the Communist Tudeh Party or by the religious-fundamentalist followers of Mullah Kashani. A lawyer, Muhammad Mussadiq, ruled for a time and forced the second Shah, Muhammad Reza, to flee the country in 1953. An armed coup restored him to power and he set out to continue the reforms started by his father. For instance, Reza had decreed the lifting of the veil in 1936.

In 1963 Muhammad gave women the right to vote and in 1975 he masterminded the Family Protection Law, not only to allow women to divorce their husbands but to allow them to challenge their husband's divorce actions, a major departure from Islamic practice.

Shah Muhammad had a great dream—to create as quickly as possible a modern industrial Muslim nation in the ancient sands of Persia. In his impetuous pursuit of industrial growth the Shah sent tens of thousands of young Iranians overseas for advanced education. Many of them stayed abroad as embittered exiles. The Shah apparently did not realize that the middle classes, which came to constitute about 25 per cent of the Iranian population, wanted increased political rights and freedom of expression as well as a share in the country's new wealth. A catalogue of the Shah's mistakes would fill pages but his greatest failing seems to have been that he forgot that he ruled an Islamic country. His second greatest mistake, in January 1978, was to allow his premier, then Jamshid Amuzegar, to cancel the 80-million-dollar annual subsidy paid to the mullahs to spend on mosques, scholarships and travel. Mullahs have no less regard for money than ordinary people and this loss deeply angered them. Since they were already scandalized by growing corruption that involved the royal family, by the jet-setting Western ways of Iran's new rich and by the Shah's apparent contempt for the true faith, they were eager for his downfall.

Like so many Islamic rulers who believe that the great ends they have set themselves justify any means, Shah Muhammad created an efficient secret police organization, Savak, to find dissidents and imprison or exile them. Many were tortured and it must be assumed that the all-powerful Shah knew about the torture.

With American encouragement, the Shah built up a large and powerful army and became "America's closest ally in the Third World," a buffer against Soviet expansion, the "policeman of the Persian Gulf" and the greatest power in Islam, with the possible exception of Turkey. It was generally believed that though other regimes might collapse the Pahlevi dynasty was impregnable.

Among those the Shah had exiled was the Ayatollah Ruhollah Khomeini, who published an article in *Impact International*, in 1971, when he was living in Iraq. The first sentence reads, "The history of Islam is a history of struggle against the monarchy." Khomeini urged the ulama to lead the fight against the Shah and to guide the workers and students. They obeyed this exhortation, partly because Khomeini gave them historical justification; he told them that neither the Prophet's son-in-law, Ali, nor his grandson, Husain, kept out of politics. The ulama had a duty to sacrifice their lives if this was necessary to defeat oppression and exploitation.

The Savak intelligence chiefs did not take Khomeini too seriously, considering him too old to cause trouble. Western leaders also thought as much and editorials in many Western newspapers asked who was Khomeini that he could take such authority to himself and how he could get away with it. The fact is, an imam can appoint himself to a position of religious authority if he has the necessary qualifications—and even if he does not have them but is willing to consult the ulama. Knowledge is much more important than piety. As a patriarchal figure of some seniority Khomeini appointed himself Muhammad's avenger.

In February 1979 Khomeini held a press conference in Paris and made a significant statement: "There is not a single true Islamic state in existence today where social justice is practiced. Our task will be to endeavor in modern history to approach this ideal as closely as is practically possible. This will take many years but I have been called, together with my religious leaders, to make a start in that direction. We are striving for the ideal society such as the Prophet himself saw it. . . ."

He passed instructions to the people by cassette tapes which were flown to Iran and played in the mosques. When he wanted violent action he gave a simple order: "Do not pay taxes, close your stores, go into the streets." Khomeini understood that successful revolutionaries need an ideology that is relevant to the hopes of the mass of the people. Shi'a Islam, with all its messianic elements—the belief in the coming, in each age, of the true heir to the Prophet, the Hidden Imam or even the Mahdi—is an inherently revolutionary creed. Khomeini exploited this, as did the Communists and Marxists for their secular ambitions.

A successful revolution also requires an organized conspiracy and, in modern times, a foreign base. Teheran could not have fallen within days of Khomeini's return had not the guerrilla groups—the Majahedeen and Fedayeen, armed and financed by Libya and the Palestinians —and the Tudeh Communist Party cells in the armed forces been well prepared for street fighting.

A perceptive American journalist, Stephen Rosenfeld, saw more clearly than his national leaders that Muslims were reacting violently to the pace and pressures of modernization and he was disturbed by what he saw. "The crisis in Iran conveys a chilling message that a dark new force is at work in the world . . . Islam in its particular relationship to modernization."*

Characteristically, the State security apparatus overreacted to this dark new force and made brutal, punitive attacks on whole towns and on schools, hospitals and on any place where "demonstrators" were believed to be in hiding. Many attacks by Savak thugs were made without reference to the responsible ministry. For instance, in January 1979 police and troops savagely beat academics at the Ministry of Higher Education for protesting against the Shah's policies. They gave "special attention" to six women professors, hitting them in the breast and pubic region and shouting "Harlot!" More than 20 professors were seriously injured.

At Ershard High School, East Teheran, troops and police ringed the High School after the boys, aged thirteen to eighteen, staged a mild demonstration. Then they moved through the school, shooting and beating, after which they assembled the boys and, using truncheons and rubber hoses, thrashed each one. The playground was full of blood and excrement from the terrified boys. In Mashdad troops attacked a hospital, killing two child patients and injuring five doctors. Many arrests were callously

*Washington Post, January, 1979.

arbitrary. A sixteen-year-old boy was arrested as he stood outside the front door of his home and his family spent weeks going from hospital to hospital, police station to police station, cemetery to cemetery, before they found him—alive but terrified.

Many arrests were carefully planned, especially those of writers and academics with a history of "political activism." One of the worse cases in Teheran was that of a woman sociologist who became infamous in the eyes of the administration by bringing a court case against the award of phony fail marks to anti-Shah students. She was arrested by armed men, raped and cut with a knife, then tied up and tossed from a moving car.

The great anti-Shah pro-Khomeini marches in Teheran, with more than a million people taking part, were manifestations of a true people's movement and of Islamic fervor, since it was this which kept people of disparate political beliefs together. Several times groups of Iranian youths dressed in white—the Islamic custom for burial— marched defiantly towards the Shah's soldiers chanting "Allahu Akbar"—God is Great. Other young men smeared themselves with blood and, fired by an insane religious machismo, ran towards the army's bullets, bayonets and clubs.

In desperation the Shah appointed Shahpour Bakhtiar to form a government which could create "genuine social democracy." The brave but incredibly naïve Bakhtiar was doomed from the time Khomeini opened his mouth to proclaim that "obedience to the Bakhtiar regime is obedience to Satan." Such a pronouncement was equivalent to a court death sentence.

Returning to Iran soon after the Shah had left, Khomeini made his homecoming speech in the holy city of Qum in March 1979. "I will devote the remaining one or two years of my life to reshaping Iran in the image of Muhammad . . . by the purge of every vestige of Western culture from the land. We will amend the newspapers. We will amend the radio, the television, the cinemas—all of these should follow the Islamic pattern . . . What the nation wants is an Islamic republic. Not just a republic, not a democratic republic, not a democratic Islamic republic.

Just an Islamic republic. Do not use the word 'democratic'. That is Western and we do not want it."

On another occasion Khomeini said: "The Islamic state is free of all despotism. It is a constitutional state, but not in the modern sense where the constitution is interpreted by parliament or public representative bodies. The Islamic state is a constitutional state in the sense that those charged with running it are bound by the rules and conditions laid down by the Koran and Sunna." Iran's zealots had long wanted total control over that which they most hated, the Constitution. An ayatollah described it as "sinful." It could hardly be anything else, he explained, since it had ideas borrowed from such "atrociously decadent" societies as Britain, Belgium, Switzerland and the United States. Khomeini and his lieutenants were in no mood for compromise—if only because compromise is not sanctioned by Islam. With a bitterness against the monarchy fostered by fifteen years' frustration in exile, the old ayatollah pursued his vendetta through to its climax of total triumph and revenge, regardless of the cost in human terms.

The swift creation of a cult of personality around the ayatollah showed how vulnerable Islamic society is to a demagogue and therefore how volatile and unstable that society can be. Ayatollah Khomeini was at once proclaimed as *the* Imam"; the crowds strained forward to draw *barak*—spiritual power—by touching him. Clothes rubbed against his clothes are now treated as sacred relics. Yet Khomeini was so aloof, so grim as to be almost not human; apparently preferring the awe and fear he inspired.

The many Iranians who wondered what an Islamic republic might be were not kept long in doubt. Within weeks they noted that they had the same surveillance, the same press censorship, crowded prisons and secretive rule—but now all this was theocratic rather than autocratic. Under the new laws several youths were forced to marry girls with whom, in the excitement of revolutionary fervor, they had "had relations."

More seriously, it was clear that an Islamic republic exacts revenge. "Like a genie let out of its bottle," read a

London *Daily Telegraph* editorial on March 14, 1979, "Iran's revolution swirls about in shapes that are ugly, bizarre and confusing." The newspaper was referring to executions the previous day of supporters of the Shah, shot by firing squads after travesties of trial by "Islamic revolutionary courts." The *Telegraph* found these courts as "ominous as they are shocking." The ominous aspect was that the day's batch of victims included, for the first time, a parliamentary deputy and two senior pro-Shah journalists. The paper called the killings "cold-blooded quasi-judicial murders" and blamed Khomeini.

The case of former Prime Minister Amir Abbas Hoveida shows the vengeful lengths to which Islamic zealots will go. Hoveida, who served as Prime Minister under the Shah for thirteen years, was by far the most important official of the old regime to stand trial for his life. Ironically, he had been jailed by the Shah on charges of corruption and this made him easy to find by the Komiteh, the powerful group of activists around Khomeini.

Many aspects of the court procedure were disturbing. A man known as Hakem-a-Shari—one who rules according to religious law—sat in place of honor as the evidence was given. It was his decision on whether execution should be carried out, giving his reasons according to Islamic law. The court sat in a room normally used as a training center in Qasr Prison, Teheran's main jail. The five judges were not named though it is known that all were lawyers who had been imprisoned by the Shah; they might therefore be prejudiced against anybody who had worked for the Shah.

The trial began after midnight, with about 200 members of the "general public" crammed into the small, whitewashed room. Hoveida sat on a chair in front of the court, and, groggy from a sleeping pill he had taken earlier, he protested that he had been promised an afternoon session. The presiding judge said, "Day or night makes no difference because this is a revolutionary court." He then read a seventeen-point indictment; with each of the charges carrying the death penalty. They ranged from general corruption to spying for the West and smuggling heroin from France. But the most chilling and unanswerable accusation was "Entering into battle against God and his emissaries."

The Khomeini-appointed Prime Minister, Mehdi Bazargan, was appalled by this Inquisition-like charge and appealed directly to Khomeini who granted a reprieve to Hoveida. It did not last long and Hoveida was shot.

It was significant that throughout the slaughters carried out by the Islamic religious courts no Islamic nation made any public protest.

Khomeini's revocation of the Family Protection Law, his abolition of co-educational schools and his diatribe against "naked women" in the government offices confirmed the worst fears of many Iranian women. They took to the street in protest, up to 15,000 parading daily in Teheran. Here some were savagely attacked and knifed by young male extremists. *Time* Magazine reported that one group of male counter-demonstrators, seeing some women standing at the windows of a Teheran office, exposed their genitals and shouted, "You don't want chadors, you want *this!*"

Iran's Islamic fervor threatens the nation's minorities. The Bahais are the most vulnerable since they have been most persecuted in the past. The Bahais preach international government and the brotherhood of man cutting across national borders, which they would like to see abolished. Iran's 300,000 Bahais are scapegoats for all ills. They are accused of having collaborated with the Shah and growing rich as a result, and they are charged with being agents of "world Zionism" because their administrative center is in Haifa, Israel. In fact it was in Haifa before the State of Israel was founded. Finally they are "agents of American imperialism" because their faith has spread to the United States. In December 1978 400 Bahai homes were damaged, looted or burned down in Shiraz province; in Amerbaijan two men were killed and quartered, the religious center was razed and 80 homes looted. At Hamadan and Khormuz 150 families fled from their homes before they were attacked but lost all their possessions.

Christians form the second largest minority, about

220,000 in all. The 200,000 Armenians have suffered the most among Christians.

Iran's Jewish community of 70,000 to 80,000 has been in the country for 27 centuries and at first wanted to believe itself safe because it is well integrated. But from fear of the Islamic zealots more than 18,000 left in the six months before Khomeini's return to Iran. The remainder fear that the PLO, which now has an office in Teheran—the former Israeli consulate—will incite Iranians against them on the grounds that they are Zionist which, manifestly, they are not. While sympathizing with Israel many Iranian Jews have no aspirations towards living there and know no more about Zionism than most of their Iranian neighbors.

The first direct blow against the Jews fell in May 1979 with the execution of a prominent Jew, Habib Elghanian, a plastics merchant in his sixties. He was an early victim of the PLO plot to induce Khomeini's administration to turn against the Jewish community. Elghanian was charged with spying for Israel, though this is extremely unlikely—until the revolution Israel had a consulate in Teheran and its attachés were in close touch with Iran's armed forces. Elghanian was without political connections and was in no position to spy about anything other than plastics. He was also said to have solicited funds for the Israeli army which made him "an accomplice in murderous air-raids against innocent Palestinians." In fact, Elghanian had merely contributed to Jewish charities within the Iranian Jewish community. The "Popular Islamic Police" has such a long blacklist of wealthy Jews that years will be needed to investigate their money, "corruption" and possible association with the Shah.

The smallest religious community, with 30,000 Zoroastrians, is Iran's oldest community. Their religion is one of tolerance but they, too, fear the new Islam.

In a revolutionary Islamic state nobody is safe. The Economist noted (May 12, 1979) that "Iranians have an obsession with blood matched only by their conviction that all-embracing plots and conspiracies represent the natural order of society."

The comment was almost prophetic. Before revolution was two months old it had spawned the Forghan Fighters, a clandestine terrorist group which quickly claimed notoriety by murdering General Muhammad Gharani and Ayatollah Motahari, both close allies of Khomeini, and wounding other leaders. Forghan is a Persian word meaning "the distinction between truth and falsehood" and it is also an alternative name for the Koran. The group portrays itself as a fundamentalist sect which wants the basic teachings of Islam to be implemented but is opposed to "the dictatorship of the mullahs." The ruling Revolutionary Council asserts that Forghan is a Communist group, though this is not remotely likely. Yet another theory is that Forghan is a cover for a faction within the Revolutionary Council killing its chief opponents as a prelude to taking over power. To students of Islam it is just another manifestation of the bloody violence which is endemic to Islamic politics.*

Indirectly Khomeini himself had incited Forghan, for he had said, just before Motahari's murder, "Criminals should not be tried, they should be killed. I am sorry that there is still Western sickness among us." He was referring to the sickness which demands that even "obvious" criminals should have a fair trial. Forghan regarded Motahari and other of its victims as "criminals."

The Iranian revolution is not finished. There may be a phase in which the Khomeini experiment will disintegrate under the pressure of Leftist groups. The pro-Marxist Fedayeen People's Party wants a "workers' republic," a people's army and nationalized enterprises run by workers' committees. The National Democratic Front, organized by a Cambridge-educated lawyer, Matine-Daftary, wants yet another system whose connection with "democracy" in the Western sense will be minimal.

Iran has "moderate" ayatollahs such as Shariat-Ma-

---

*At the height of the juridical killings, horse-racing, which had ceased with the arrival of the revolution, was allowed to start again. Ayatollah Motahari announced that study showed that the Koran did not forbid horse-racing. Betting was also acceptable provided that race-track bettors paid a fee to join a "club." This creates the fiction that they are betting among themselves and not against outsiders, which would be against Islamic law.

dari, but in joining with Khomeini they started a process they cannot stop. All successful revolutionaries are eager to export revolution. Khomeini's acolytes will obey his wishes to see Jordan, Saudi Arabia and Morocco "ridden" of their kings and lesser states of their ruling princes.

Khomeini explicitly invited other Islamic peoples to stage their own revolution. "By following our example other countries will free themselves from the clutches of colonialism," he said in several broadcasts. Early in 1979 active cells of Khomeini followers were found in Kuwait, Qatar, Bahrain, Oman; Khomeini's aides had established several hundred religious "study groups," most of which were active in propagating Khomeini's fundamentalist tenets; a few were stockpiling arms, notably in Kuwait. The "husseiniyah," or study group, is an old-established institution in Iran and among other Shi'a communities. Because they are accepted they make ideal cells for subversion.

Iran now has a Deputy Prime Minister for Revolutionary Affairs, Ibrahim Yazdi, who has stifled Iran's press and been direct in his encouragement to other Islamic militants. "From now on all Islamic movements that were dormant or apologetic in their approach to change or action will come out in the open in the Muslim world."*

TURKEY   Deeply Rooted Discontent

When Kemal Ataturk brought the first Turkish Republic into being in 1923 and made it a secular state he denounced Islam as "the rules and theories of an immoral Arab sheikh" and banned the pilgrimage to Mecca. To emphasize that henceforth Turkey would not be dominated by religion Ataturk abolished the Caliphate and the Ministry of Religious Affairs and unified the schools under a secular Ministry of Education. European civil and criminal codes replaced the Shari'a and, in 1928, Latin letters were substituted for the Arabic script. Dress was modernized by Government decree and even imams were not allowed to wear their robes in public.

*Time Magazine, April 16, 1979.

By its support of the United Nations action in Korea (1950) its admission to NATO (1952) and leadership in concluding the Baghdad Treaty (re-labeled the Central Treaty Organization) Turkey became firmly committed to the West. Transition to democracy was interrupted by an army coup in 1960 but in 1961 a Second Republic was proclaimed, with democratic-parliamentary government.

In the 1970s, despite much general liberalism, Turkey has suffered from tremendous problems, many of them foisted on it by ignorant Western leaders who knew little and cared less about the Turkish people. The U.S. and NATO have viewed Turkey in strategic and military terms and have paid no attention to economic needs and to social and religious attitudes.

The reaction of the Western media in apparently siding with the Greek Cypriots rather than the Turkish Cypriots has made even Turkish intellectuals believe that Western Europe is prejudiced against Turkey because it is a Muslim country—whereas Greece is Christian. To suppose that European politicians and journalists are animated by this sort of Christian sentiment is naïve but the Turks find it difficult to see any other explanation for the way in which the U.S. stopped military aid—over Cyprus—to one of its staunchest allies.

Ataturk's attempt to make a secular state of Turkey has failed, partly because he apparently did not understand the need of his basically peasant people for religion. His secular state gave them much material support but no emotional and spiritual security. He could not kill Islam, he merely manacled it. Now it has struggled free and given birth to a National Survival (Islamic) Party, whose leader, Nejmuddin Erbakan, depicts the West, Christian and Jew alike, as the common enemy of the Muslim countries. By doing this he believes he can mobilize the strong religious sentiment of the Turks and arouse sympathy in the Arab world—with all the economic benefits this might produce. As a Deputy Prime Minister he is in a good position to tell his people that "NATO, the Common Market and the West in general are inspired by the spirit of the Crusades."

Uneasy in intellect and conscience, many Turks have

renounced Ataturk's anti-Islamic reforms, the more de-
vout or militant finding refuge and stimulation in the
Tarika brotherhood or the mystic sect of Tasawwuf. The
Justice Party came into being and gained support largely
on its promise to abolish the ban imposed by Kemal
Ataturk on making the Muslim pilgrimage.

Islamic fervor, finding expression throughout Turkey,
is an expression of deeply rooted discontent with half a
century of secularism and of worry about inflation and
unemployment.

Escalation of political violence has reached a dangerous peak and it raises serious doubts about the nation's
future. The murders of university professors, school
teachers, judges and army officers are part of a campaign
of terror; more than 1,000 people died during 1978 and
the monthly figures were rising. The terrorists are of
mixed ideologies, from extreme right wing to extreme left
wing, but a good many are Islamic zealots. Sectarian
rioting—Sunnis and Shi'as are at each other's throats—is
endemic. In December 1978 more than 100 people were
killed in sectarian fighting in Karaman Maras.

Turkey is viewed by Western optimists an an unlikely
place for Islamic fundamentalism to assert itself as force-
fully as in Iran. But this view presupposes that outside
Islamic influences will not make themselves felt in Turkey. In fact, the zealots of Libya, Iran, Iraq and the PLO
would like to see Turkey once again within the Islamic
fold. In any case, political extremists—especially the
Maoists and Leninists—who are not themselves interested
in an Islamic republic might well use religious issues to
bring down the government.

It is no comfort that the National Salvation Party lost
half its political strength between 1973 and 1977, falling
to 24 seats from 48 in the 450-seat National Assembly
and gaining only 8.5 per cent of the vote. Korkut Ozal,
the driving force of the party, has said, ominously, that
Islam does not need votes to succeed in its intention to
"restore Turkey to its pure Islamic condition."

The government affirms that Turkey will remain within NATO but it has nevertheless sought treaties with
Arab states. Almost certainly the dagger of Islam will

next be drawn in Turkey; how soon it will be drawn and how bloodily depends on the understanding and sympathy of the U.S. and of the European countries. This could avert catastrophe.

ALGERIA   Triumph and Tragedy

Algeria differs from other Arab Muslim nations in that it has found a way of using the best the West can offer while remaining genuinely Islamic. Anyone who spent time in Algeria during its war with France (1954–1962) knows the great part Islam played in arousing national sentiment. It crystallized the vast but vague discontent of the masses into the precise national pattern which the leaders of the Front de Libération Nationale (FLN) wished it to take. Mosque attendances increased dramatically from 1955 on, especially as the revolution gained support in rural districts that had been indifferent or hostile.

Ahmed Ben Bella, Algeria's first prime minister, and other Algerian leaders always insisted that their one-party constitution is a modern version of the Islamic umma (society) inspired by tribal conditions, then adapted to city life and directed by Allah's will. Such an adaptation showed an unusual willingness to compromise and it was opposed by the fundamentalist religious leaders as blasphemous.

The political leaders, first Ben Bella and then Houari Boumedienne, calmed the zealots and explained to them, as well as to foreigners, that the Algerian Islamic society was, with its adaptations, strong enough to resist Communism. Nevertheless, the Algerians admired Fidel Castro, they were fascinated by the Chinese experiment in Communism and they were increasingly dependent on Soviet economic aid.

Under its 1963 consitution Algeria became an Islamic state. The conception was that the constitution should represent a spiritual, economic and moral consensus—not of the whole people but of the élite—those best able to exercise judgment.

Ben Bella, and no less Boumedienne, said that in their

ideal Islamic state the vote of the majority rules—but the majority had to be guided by the enlightened minority, the FLN Party. Contested elections could not be permitted "because Islam does not believe in the collective infallibility of the incompetent nor in the majority of the ignorant," in Ben Bella's words. Islam could not tolerate organized opposition in the sense of a rival political party, but the populace could ratify the decision or choice made by the élite or they could denounce and reject it.

Colonel Benjedid Chadly, who succeeded to the presidency in February 1979, after Boumedienne's death, will keep Algeria firmly socialist, centrally run and anti-Israel and he will support such "liberation movements" as the Palestine Liberation Organization and the Saharan Polisario. He is dedicated, like his predecessor and colleagues, to rapid industrialization and economic development. They do not fear an Iran-type revolution, though there is growing discontent among the people about the shortage of consumer goods after fifteen years' investment in heavy industry. With Europe now closed to additional Algerian "guest workers" the nation also faces serious unemployment. Boumedienne had a policy of close cooperation with Western nations and Chadly will intensify this policy. Algeria wants to play the leading role in North Africa, and the French, who closely monitor Algeria's performance, believe that this is likely.

But Algeria's enlightenment does not extend to women. It is possible that no other Muslim women are so badly treated as in Algeria. Journalist Anthony McDermott wrote, "Socialist Algeria with its planning for heavy industry and its admirable social services is forward-looking, Islamic Algeria looks backward to reinforce Arab traditions."* He is referring to Algerian women, whose plight has been described by an Algerian sociologist writing under the pseudonym "Mahl" in *People.*†

Their fathers, brothers or paternal uncles, and later their husbands and sons, decide everything for them,

*Arab Women, a Minority Groups report, 1976.
†Organ of the International Planned Parenthood Association, vol. 2, No. 5, 1975.

and manage their property. If the man abuses his authority, the woman will become his slave, in the strictest economic sense of the word ... If he is good, she will have to give thanks every day of her life for the good fortune that has placed her in the hands of such a good master, for it is from her master that she derives her social legitimacy. A woman alone—a widow or a single woman without male relatives—finds it almost impossible to obtain recognition from authority, for example in getting a flat through the state bureaucracy ... Many such women lost their men in the liberation struggle but others are similarly placed as a result of repudiation, which allows a man to send away his wife without giving her freedom to remarry and thereby regain legitimacy by means of a legal divorce ..."

The most sober picture of ordinary Algerian people in modern times is painted by Dr. Ian Young in his book *The Private Life of Islam,* the record of Dr. Young's service in a large hospital in rural Kabylia. *Newsweek,* reviewing the book, noted that, "On one level the book is an almost unbearable catalogue of horror stories, of women needlessly butchered on operating tables, of brutally torn wombs, of needlessly stillborn babies, of suffering casually inflicted on a primitive, uncomprehending passive group of women ... the Algerian hospital staff seems more intent on paying lip service to 'Muslim Socialist Algeria' than in caring for the neglected patients."*

Young's descriptions of family life are perceptive and sensitive and honest. His stories are shocking but he does not set out to shock. He tells of bleeding teenage girls brought to the hospital with lacerated vaginas after being subjected to brutal intercourse by their husbands. A 40-year-old bridegroom said to Young, "There's nothing wrong with the girl!" as he forcibly removed his hemorrhaging and terrified sixteen-year-old wife from the hospital. Husbands refuse to give blood for the dying wives.

Hospital life reflects the male-dominated Algerian soci-

*Allen Lane, London, 1974.

ety and Dr. Young, in effect, is indicting the Algerian government for its indifference to women's suffering. The *Newsweek* reviewer believes that "There has never been a book as stark and factual as Young's" and he considers that its most disturbing aspect reveals the "insidious dangers of totalitarianism."

By sheer will and tenacity some young women got themselves into universities and in 1979 a quarter of the students and 40 per cent of the country's medical practitioners were women. The few who have become lawyers are so eloquent that they often win their cases by leaving their male opponents literally speechless. Male lawyers dislike having to face a woman in court in case she wins; this is an afront to their ego.

Going to college can have terrible consequences for a girl. When she returns home she may be forced into veiling and an arranged marriage. Girls have been known to commit suicide rather than submit to such marriages; Fadela M'rabet notes that in just one year at least 175 such suicides occurred.

Even the professional women are not truly emancipated but in its confrontation with religious fundamentalists the small female intelligentsia is well represented by the National Union of Algerian Women (UNFA) which has an impressive paper membership of 160,000. It has nothing to be pleased about with the rise of prominence of Colonel Muhammad Salah Yahiaoui, the vice-president in charge of domestic issues. He told the National Union of Algerian Women at their fourth congress that they were deluding themselves if they expected to be given equal rights with men. Like most Algerian men, Yahiaoui considers UNFA as an irritant rather than a pacemaker for social change.

Of Algeria's population of 16.3 million 9.5 million are women—and 80 per cent of them are illiterate. UNFA's educated young women describe themselves as "the sacrifice generation" because they have gained so little personal liberty from Algeria's own liberation. But their daughters may reap fuller benefits, they say, and eventually, so may the great mass of oppressed Algerian womanhood. Weighed against the sad plight of these women Algeria's technological advances hardly turn the scales.

LEBANON   *Dagger Dripping Blood*

It is said in Beirut that a Maronite priest delivered a sermon in which he advised his Christian congregation, for their own safety, to think of themselves as Arabs. A woman accosted him after the service and told him the story of the lunatic who, thinking he was a grain of wheat, was afraid of the hens. He was treated and cured. "That's fine," he said, "so I am not a grain of wheat. But do the hens know that?" This twisted story has some relevance to the dilemma of Lebanon, the country which has suffered more grievously than any other Middle East nation in recent years. Yet Lebanon was often presented as an example of the ideal where followers of the two greatest world faiths lived in balanced numbers and shared the responsibility of government. It was said that if Lebanon could achieve this stability, other nations could. What went wrong? The political-social-religious framework of Lebanon is complex but its elements can be clearly discerned. At the start of the civil war in April 1975 the total population was about 2,000,000 in seventeen different sects and religions, plus the 400,000 Palestinians, mostly Muslim. The largest religious community until recent years was the Maronite Christian sect, Catholics who recognize the authority of the Pope. Maronites refuse to call themselves Arabs, especially in the political sense; as Lebanese, they say, they are a distinct race.

The Sunni Muslims, the next largest group, are a major branch of Islam with their main centers in Beirut, Tripoli and the Bekaa Valley. They are Arabs first, Lebanese second. About equally strong in numbers are the Shi'a Muslims. Located mainly in southern Lebanon (before the civil war) the Shi'as are the poorest Lebanese and have the highest birthrate.

A significant group are the Druze, an heretical Islamic sect. Druzes will sometimes concede that they are Muslims but other Muslims do not usually accept them. A mountain people, the Druze can be violent and ruthless but for centuries they lived closely and peacefully, inter-mingled with the Maronites.

Orthodox Christians were, at the beginning of 1975, scattered throughout Lebanon and well integrated into Lebanese society, as were the Armenian Christians, who tried to remain neutral in the civil war despite a tradition-al electoral alliance with the Maronites. Overall, Muslims outnumbered Christians. There was thus a delicate reli-gious balance, recognized by a constitutional arrangement under which the President would always be a Maronite, the Prime Minister a Sunni and the President of the National Assembly a Shi'a. Other government posts were on a 6-5 basis, Christians predominating over Muslims. The system worked well enough and any conflict was between poor Christians and poor Muslims "against" rich Christians and rich Muslims.

The presence of the Palestinians changed all this. Be-fore 1970 Lebanon had about 200,000 Palestinian refu-gees. By 1975 the figure was between 400,000 and 450,000. This increase was caused partly by the Jordan Civil War of 1970 when King Hussein's army drove out of Jordan large numbers of Palestinian terrorists. But the greater part of the increase was engineered by the Syrians and the Palestine Liberation Organization, encouraged by the Soviet Union. The additional Palestinians were smug-gled into Lebanon to put an intolerable burden on Leba-non's capacity to absorb them and so provide cause for friction which could, in turn, be exploited for political ends. The French Government's investigator, Couve de Murville, reported these facts to the French cabinet.

The Lebanese had not imagined that the original Pales-tinians would become a problem. The plan was to assim-ilate them into Lebanon and, with United Nations help, good homes and settlements were built. But Egyptians and Syrian agents incited the Palestinians to destroy these homes; by keeping these people in squalid camps they could more effectively exploit them. Late in the 1960s the Palestinians became a state within a state. Their terrorists were aggressive and many groups made their headquarters in Beirut. They continually harassed not only the Israeli "enemy" but the very people who had taken them in, the Lebanese. On Apil 13, 1975 a carload of Palestinians sped through a Christian area of Beirut and opened fire on a group of people leaving a church service. This began the civil war and by the end of 1976 40,000 Lebanese were dead, many in horrible massacres, and another 200,000 had been wounded. Probably another 10,000 died between 1976 and 1979. At the height of the fighting in 1976 Salah Khalaf, the most influential leader of Fatah—the fighting wing of the PLO—declared that the war aim of the Palestinians was the conquest of the whole Christian north of Lebanon.

Officially, the war ended when an Arab peace-keeping force, mostly of Syrians, occupied Lebanon. Originally the Syrians moved in to break the Lebanese Left and the Palestinians, who, by Syrian assessment, were becoming too strong. The Syrians were thus in alliance with the Christians but this union lasted only a few months. Soon the Christians found that they had two enemies—the Palestinians plus the Syrians. They also found that they had only one ally, Israel.

The southern and northern Christian areas are separated by large regions controlled by either the Palestinians or Syrians so it was more difficult for Israel to help the northern group. Through Junieh, the one port open to these Christians, the Israelis supplied them with the necessities of life as well as with arms.

Foreign observers on the spot have been in no doubt of the crisis facing Lebanese Christians. American journalist Maurice Carr wrote in May 1978, "Incontestably, about Lebanon the world at large has looked the other way, as is customary when genocide is on the agenda, whether the martyrs are Armenians, Jews, Biafrans, Kurds, Cambodians, white, black, yellow, believers in the one invisible God, or heathens."

Genocide may be too strong a word but massacre is commonplace. The only difference between one slaughter and the next is the number of victims. In March 1977 there was the massacre of Christians in the villages of Mazraat al-Shouf, Baruk, Maaser al-Shouf, Betnat and Kafar Nabrekh, when about 130 men, women and children and the old were killed indiscriminately with axes, iron bars or by knifing. Several thousand Christians fled from the Shouf Highlands to the Christian settlement areas in the north. A greater number of people were killed in the recurrent Syrian shellings of Beirut.

Sections of the world's press also saw the dangers. The London *Guardian* on July 16, 1978, referred to "something of a massacre" on the Christian population in Beirut. "This has something to do—no one is quite sure what—with taming the armed-to-the teeth Christian militias ... It also has to do with taking revenge on the particular militia whose members recently killed a Lebanese friend of the Syrian president's brother. If that sounds to you like an insubstantial set of reasons to justify the mass slaughter of civilians we could not agree more."

The main reason must be destruction of the Christians because they resent the occupation of their country by the Syrians plus the important political fact that the Christian Lebanese do not want their country used as a springboard of war against Israel. They want peace. The apparent indifference of most Muslim Arabs to the fate of the Christian Arabs is complete. Nor have the Muslims been alone in their apathy; it took six days of Syrian artillery fire in Beirut to draw a public word of concern from President Carter and the UN Secretary-General, Kurt Waldheim. Israel's interest in the Lebanese Christians is obviously not entirely humanitarian. Surrounded by enemies, it pays for Israel to have the Lebanese Christians as friends on its northern border. But whatever Israel's motives, the fact of humanitarian help is undeniable.

Beshir Gemayel, the young commander-in-chief of the Christian militias in Lebanon, has made it clear that the younger generation of Lebanese Christians want to survive as independent Christians in a free democratic state, not as subjects under Islamic rule or as third-class citizens in a Communist people's republic ruled by Palestinians, Syrians and the radical Lebanese Left.

Harald Vock in his book *The Lebanese War** says, "The determination of the young Lebanese Christians to

*Hurst & Co., London, 1978.

defend their freedom and their Christian values gives them considerable political strength in their difficult struggle for survival." Vocke says that independent Western reporters in Beirut have long been afraid to cable the truth about Lebanon, hence the world is kept in ignorance of the sad facts of Lebanese life. "Like the embassies," Vocke says, "the Western newspapers and broadcasting networks had their offices in the Palestinian-controlled western area of Beirut. The central post office is also situated there, so it was from West Beirut that these correspondents could cable, telephone or teleprint their reports. Just as the Palestinians had terrorized the diplomats by the murder of the American ambassador, so they intimidated the Western press correspondents by the murder of the permanent correspondent of the Paris daily, *Le Monde* . . . Also the Belgian press photographer Marc Thirion was kidnapped and never heard of again."

After these events, Vocke suggests, all Western correspondents felt themselves threatened by the Palestinians. They began to take up more and more the language of the Palestinian terrorists "in order to gain the Palestinians' favor and protect themselves." Western action in Lebanon has been minimal, also for good pragmatic reasons. The Western leaders fear that by intervening they may arouse Arab anger which could show itself by cutting off oil exports. The United States has an additional worry —that its involvement could lead to Soviet counter-involvement. In fact, the Soviet's part as agent-provocateur in the Lebanese tragedy is already great.

Restoration of a truly "free Lebanon" will happen only when the President is able to re-establish his authority over the whole country with a new non-sectarian army, and the Syrian and UN peace-keeping troops can withdraw. But it is doubtful whether the Muslim leaders will for long tolerate the Christian part of the population which refuses to call itself Arab.

TUNISIA   *Victim of the mullahs*

While the state of Tunisia is not one of the important Islamic counties in prestige, military power or militancy, since 1977 it has become a likely victim of Islamic Republicanism. The change has been dramatic.

Until January 1977 Tunisia was an island of stability and progress in an ocean of Islamic-world unrest. In terms of per-capita income it was one of Africa's five richest countries and its gross national product between 1956—the year of independence from France—and 1976 increased from 920 million dollars to 2,974 million.

Illiteracy is lower than in most Islamic countries and a large proportion of the budget is spent on education. For an Islamic country the emancipation of women has proceeded smoothly; the country even has a comprehensive family planning program.

Also until January 1977 Tunisia's remarkable economic achievements were matched by its political peace—though this was partly the result of there being only one party.

Then came a shortage of jobs and a sense of frustration among the young, who expected more of the state and its President, Habib Bourguiba, than they could possibly offer. During 1976 an increasing number of student demonstrations and wildcat strikes occurred; Left-wing activists accused the government of consolidating foreign interests while the fundamentalists, incited by Gaddafi, demanded a "return to Islam." He engineered an abortive plot by Palestinians to assassinate Bourguiba and expelled its 15,000 Tunisian workers.

In January 1977 riots broke out in Tunis. The army was called into the streets and troops opened fire on the rioters. More than 100 people died and several hundred were injured. Martial law was declared and about 1,000 trade unionists and students were arrested. The day of rioting became known as "Black Thursday."

Encouraged by this blood conflict, Muslim provocateurs from Libya, Saudi Arabia, Iraq and Algeria moved in to provoke more trouble and bring down Bourguiba, long detested among the fundamentalists as too moderate to be a Muslim leader. One of his gravest "crimes" is that he has tolerated Christian and Jewish minorities. Also, he has aligned Tunisia with the United States, France and Italy economically and politically. In Islamic eyes his successor-elect Hedi Nouira, for many years the Prime Minister, is not much better than Bourguiba as a Muslim. The priests object to the large numbers of tourists traveling to Tunisia; these foreigners, they say, are spreading "dangerous social diseases." Since the Iranian revolution the stresses within Tunisia have become even more intense, and younger Tunisians are advocating revolution to rid the country of "Western influences." In fact, the only obvious Western influence is the French language, which is spoken by large numbers of Tunisians. Bourguiba may have been trying to introduce Tunisia to the twentieth century too fast for a conservative people to accept without some doubt and confusion. Confusion, aggravated by skilful Islamic agitators, is a raw material of revolution. The agitators, who include mullahs paid by Gaddafi, are trying to sell the idea that the administration is pro-Israeli and therefore anti-Koranic. Bourguiba and his associates, with a political realism inherited from the French, regard the obsession with Israel as an irrelevancy, an Arab "sickness."

16

AFRICA—DRIVE FOR CONVERTS

In 1960 a *Newsweek* contributor wrote with direct and simple bluntness, "Christianity in Africa is a force done with . . . As for Islam, it is strong and growing . . . Our best policy would be to cooperate with Islam."*

Seven years later John K. Cooley found that "A great Muslim tide is sweeping over most of the African continent and shows no sign of ebbing."† Cooley's prophecy was accurate; so great has been the tide that according to UN estimates Islam is making up to ten million converts a year in pagan Africa, which is many times faster than the Christian church can bring in converts.

Christianity is suspect as the white man's religion and as countries throw off their colonial status they are tempted to cut adrift a religion closely associated in their minds— though not necessarily in fact—with imperialism. It is true enough that Christian missionaries were never far behind the traders and they were nearly always ahead of the administrators. For the moment Africans have forgotten that it was the Arab slavers who first brought the word of Islam to Africa. Their penetration was brutal, destructive and dominant. Europeans began their mad

---

*Dr. Garland Hopkins, October 3, 1960.
†*Baal, Christ and Mohammed,* John Murray, 1967.

scramble for Africa little more than a century ago; before that Muslims were the masters.

Now mullahs from al-Azhar are spreading Islam throughout Africa while Gaddafi's agents accompany them to hand out money in exchange for allegiance to the "Arab cause," though their descriptions about what this cause might be are more inflammatory than informative.

In parts of Africa, particularly south of the Sahara, Muslims have to share their country with non-Muslims. Sometimes they are minorities and they resent the secularization brought in by the West which they feel is undermining their religion. Muslim policy then is to maintain the essentials of their religion, such as the rule of the Shari'a, family law and their own education. Since this education is almost wholly religious it is backward in contrast with the education given in secular schools developed by Christian missions. The tension between Muslim and Christian can become unbearable and sometimes it reaches breaking point. It is one of the reasons for armed conflict in Chad—more than 50 per cent Muslim.

Muslim missionaries and "advisers" are busy in many places, and their ascendancy over their Christian counterparts is evident. For instance, the influence of Christian churches appears to be receding among Zulus but, with the Koran translated into Zulu, Islam is vigorous. During 1978 leading members of America's Black Muslim Movement visited the Republic of South Africa to encourage the spread of Islam, where for the moment its followers are mainly Coloreds (the South African term for people of mixed black and white descent), Malays and Indians.

The ethical code of Islam is admired because of its stress on the equality and unity of all Muslims; knowing little or nothing of Islam in practice the Africans have yet to discover that this ideal often falls very short of its aim. Another attraction is that Islam makes the black man the brother of the incomparable champion boxer Muhammad Ali—the most influential Islam convert in history—and it connects him with the fabulous wealth and power of the Arab countries. Circumcision and an aversion to pork fit in with the black man's traditional way of life and polygamy is an immense appeal.

John Osman, BBC reporter stationed in Africa says:*

One reason for the continuing appeal of Islam in Africa is that millions of African men still feel more at home with a number of wives rather than just one ... Muslim missionaries, with the backing of Arab governments, stress the horrors of the old West African slave trade. And there are now few Christian missionaries to remind them of the appalling inhumanity of the Arab trade in Negro slaves. Whole history books and text books have been re-written to stress the Muslim and often left wing viewpoint to the West. It's the attack on the West which is the sole link between Muslim zealots and Marxist dogmatists.

In many African countries Islam is particularly attractive to the black man in search of an individual identity. Linked with this comes a feeling of power and national pride and a vision of independence, wealth and self-reliance. Islam gives the Muslim a feeling of superiority over the West, which propaganda proclaims to be "decadent with its adultery, gambling, abuse of alcohol and pitiful indecisiveness." Islam makes no great demands either. The basic requirement is nothing more than the recital of the *shahada*—"There is no god but Allah and Muhammad is His messenger."

Yet like Christianity before it, Islam finds difficulties in African penetration. For example, the Islamic calendar follows the moon year which is out of gear with the African agricultural year following the sun. Islamic society is paternal while many African societies are matrilineal. A serious problem is that while men often completely accept Islam many women continue the pagan religion. They somehow understand that their position in Islam lends itself only to marginal involvement.

In internal and international political terms Islam's influence is much more significant than its effect on the lives of individuals. Statements of the late 1960s that

*In a BBC program on Islam, March 1979.

common allegiance to Islam plays little part in political relationships in Africa now make no sense. Through Islamic propaganda Muslim Afro-Arab solidarity is growing; the main propaganda technique has been to link the African Muslims and the Arab Muslims by providing them with a joint focus against Israel. Israel has given much help to the African countries but Muslim propaganda has smeared this away as a form of colonialism. In any case, Saudi Arabia is now a major aid donor in Africa and this heavy practical support naturally buys compliance. Some non-Islam countries such as Kenya, and the Congo, get Saudi aid, and it is no coincidence that the traveling mullahs are operating there.

The influence of Islam is typified in Mozambique where the biggest of the ethnic groups, the Muslim Makuas, have always been in resistance to the Frelimo Movement of President Machel. The Makuas live mainly in the northern provinces and constitute about 40 per cent of the population. Upset by Frelimo indoctrination of their children through the education system, the Muslims only need help from outside to rise against Machel, and they are confident of getting this help in time.

In world strategic terms the West must come to terms with what must be an unpalatable fact to many Western leaders. Three of the most important zones of Africa are Muslim-held—the Straits of Gibraltar on the Moroccan coastline, the Suez Canal–Red Sea region, the Horn of Africa. While the countries which have coastlines on the vital waterways remain friendly to the West the risk of their being cut is slight. But after the wild swing of Iran from friend to enemy no friendship can be taken for granted.

Dr. Garland Hopkins' advice in *Newsweek* to "cooperate" with Islam may be sound—but the terms need to be carefully negotiated.

17

UNEASY COURTSHIP—SOVIET AND ISLAM

During 1978 and 1979 newspapers and magazines ran a flurry of stories with headings such as MARCH OF ISLAM BREEDS FEAR FOR MOSCOW (*Daily Telegraph,* April 4, 1979), WAVES OF MUSLIM UPHEAVAL FELT IN USSR (*Christian Science Monitor,* April 23, 1979), and USSR AIM: TO FIGHT MOSLEM INFLUENCE (*To the Point International,* April 14, 1978).

Not since President Sadat threw his Russian military advisers out of Egypt in 1972–3 had so much attention been given to Soviet-Islam relations. With the revolution in Iran the world's press made much of the Soviet Union's own Muslim republics and population, probably 50 million of them, with some demographers projecting 100 million by the end of the century.

Just how the Communists will cope with revolutionary, militant Islam is one of the most fascinating questions of modern times. Muslims outside the Soviet Union believe that in time Allah and his warriors will destroy the Communist empire as they believe He destroyed the Christian Crusaders. From Islamic "democracies" or "social democracies" on Russia's southern sweep it is quite possible for zealous evangelism to sweep across the border into the politically repressed Soviet Muslim states, creating great problems for Soviet leadership.

Soviet flirtation with various Arab countries has been going on since the 1950s and Communist leaders had considered themselves by 1972 in practically a married state with Egypt, after seventeen years of strenuous exertion and huge investments. Then Sadat pronounced his divorce. The Soviet suffered a massive expulsion of its personnel and advisers. This was a curtailment of Russian expansion in Africa unequaled in modern history— by the Muslin Arabs, a new source of world power. After an attempted coup in Sudan in 1971 Sudanese communists were also suppressed and Soviet military advisers were expelled. The Soviet Union has since recovered from this setback and now, directly or through its surrogate, Cuba, controls much of *Christian* Africa.

To compensate for the loss of Egypt the Soviets more assiduously wooed Syria, Iraq, Libya, Algeria, the Yemens and Afghanistan, with varying degrees of success. Since the lates 1960s the Soviet Union has also had strong connections with the PLO and some of its terrorist branches.

Many Western leaders have convinced themselves that Islam and Communism are so fundamentally opposed— fierce and fixed belief in God versus inflexible atheism— that the Soviet bloc and communism can never be a force in the Islamic world. Maxime Rodinson points out that as recently as 1950 the great majority of Islamic scholars, followed by many economists, political scientists and others judged the future of the Muslim world purely on the dogmas of Islam. Their conclusion was that as the Muslim's values were of a sacred character they could not be attracted to a socialist ideology such as Marxism. Yet by the mid-sixties socialist ideology had influenced all Muslim countries. Communism itself had found many supporters. This is evident from the outlawing of Communist parties and the harassment of their members. If nothing else, these counter-measures show Muslim leaders that their flocks are not immune to the wiles of socialism/Marxism/Communism. By upbringing Muslims are great consumers of slogans and some socialist slogans appeal to them profoundly.

But slogans are not enough. In Islam there is a marked lack of interest in Soviet culture because it is completely foreign to Muslim culture in whatever Islamic country. President Nasser saw Islam as one of the basic differences between his brand of socialism and communism. Islam is central even in Arab countries with whom Russia maintains friendly relations—Algeria, Syria, Libya and Iraq. The Constitutional Declaration of Libya commences with the explicit statement that Islam is the religion of the state. Even radical south Yemen which has close links with communist countries speaks—even if not until Article 31 of the Constitution—of the preservation of its "Islamic cultural inheritance," while Article 46 declares Islam as the religion of the state.

Whatever logic is advanced for and against the power of Communism to spread in Islamic countries, statistics seem to indicate that few people are activist enough to want to join parties. Party membership as a percentage of the population in 1977 was, in Egypt .001; Algeria .002; Tunisia .002; Morocco .003; Jordan .015; Iraq .018; Sudan .019; Syria .048; Lebanon .122. But Communist influence cannot be measured by the number of members in a branch. Dedication and skill, and the quality of direction from the Soviets, count for more than numbers. Russians are experts at exploiting changes and revolutions. There is nearly always a local cell, no matter how small, on which to build.

More directly, many Muslim states have been bought by gifts of armaments. The Soviets' bonds with Syria are strong because virtually all Syria's armaments are supplied by the Soviets and its army has Russian instructors. With Egypt unavailable, the Soviets built up Syria as a substitute, a natural decision as Syria has a Mediterranean coastline. The Soviet-Libyan relationship is also harmonious on the armaments level. Gaddafi has no more tolerance for communism than he has for capitalism but he has bought tank fleets from the Soviets and equipment for military installations. Since Libya has no communist party the Soviet Union must work directly through its own agents. Libya can afford to pay cash for anything it wants so the Soviets cannot use the poverty lever to gain indirect control over the country, as they can with Syria.

In Iraq the regime of General Saddam Hussein remains friendly with Moscow but to limit Soviet influence in the region the Iraqis have cooperated quietly with the conservative Saudis. The Baghdad summit conference, in March 1979, ostensibly called to denounce the Camp David Israel-Egypt peace treaty, in reality was a Saudi-Iraqi scheme to give some support to Syria, one of the Arab states on the "front line" against Israel, and to prevent the Damascus government from becoming totally dependent on the Soviet Union for backing against the Israelis. In another triumph of pragmatism over ideology, Iraq sought the cooperation of Iran—with which it is in dispute—in order to crush the Kurdish rebellion in its northern region. The government's greatest problem is a revival of unrest among the two million Kurds, who share with their ethnic cousins in Turkey and Iran a desire for an autonomous Kurdistan. The revolution in Iran worried Iraq's ruling Ba'ath Party; its leadership is Sunni while 52 per cent of Iraq's twelve million people are Shi'as. As in Iran, the mullahs have a tradition of political activism and violent clashes between the religious dissidents and the all-Sunni army are frequent.

Iraq is most like the Soviet Union in that it has an oppressive regime which gives the people little chance of demonstrating their disapproval. A tough police state, its jails hold thousands of political prisoners. Methods of social control, of intimidation and interrogation are modeled on the Soviet Union.

Perhaps the greatest difficulty in Baghdad-Moscow relations is the enmity between the Ba'athists and the Iraqi Communists, papered over only briefly by inclusion of the party in a nominal Ba'athist-dominated ruling coalition in 1971. The regime has a pathological suspicion that the Communists' ultimate aim—like that of the Ba'athists earlier—is to seize power. While Iraq's foreign policy is avowedly anti-Israel and anti-U.S., it deals commercially with many American firms and it has good relations with several Western countries, notably France. With General Hussein's regime so clearly intent on keeping both superpowers helpful but at arms' length, chances for the Soviets to dominate Iraq are slight.

The Islamic country in which the Soviet Union regards itself as most successful is Afghanistan where, in April 1978, Soviet agents managed to help into power the Khalq (People's) Party of President Nur Muhammad Taraki and Premier Hafizullah Amin. While secular, the regime's leaders try to play safe by not mentioning the words "socialism" or "communism." Taraki wants to reform his backward nation in which 80 per cent of the people are illiterate. But mountainous Afghanistan with more than twenty different ethnic groups in its population of sixteen million is one of the least governable countries, despite massive Soviet help.

In the opinion of American journalist David DeVoss, "The only things that most Afghans seem to share, besides deep poverty and one of the world's highest illiteracy rates, are an ancient legacy of violence . . . and a powerful devotion to Islam."*

The Khalq Party is genuinely progressive in many ways. It even wants to weaken male domination by teaching women to read and in 1979 it made schooling compulsory for children over seven years of age, with the emphasis on a form of education that will lead to professional jobs. Far from welcoming this advance, many fathers refused to send their daughters to school. The Party has also made some reforms to the law—but the mullahs are angry that a civil government is to administer the law when this, traditionally, has been their role. Within a year of taking office the Taraki regime had jailed 12,000 political offenders.

Having destroyed the old oppressive landowning class, the government tackled the root causes of poverty, "the stagnation of society." But to reform society—with or without communism—the regime inevitably confronts Islam. Two extreme religious movements, the Jamiyat-i-Islami (Islamic Union) and the Hezb-i-Islami (Islamic

*Time, May 14, 1979.

Party) dedicated themselves to bringing down the government, replacing it with an Islamic republic. With strong support from Pakistan and Iran, a few thousand guerrillas can keep a large army busy for a long time, even when it has much Soviet weaponry and assistance. The mullahs pointedly recall that when in 1920 the reformer King Amanullah decided to take women out of purdah the gesture cost him his throne. The Taraki regime, in "turning against God," is likely to lose much more. Some theologians call for a "National Rescue Front"—in effect an amalgamation of Muslim parties—but as in most Islamic countries suspicion and jealously exist between rival groups. The Soviets can take some comfort from this.

But there is no consolation in the appeal by the powerful Iranian ayatollah, Shariat Medari, "to all Muslims throughout the world to support the Afghan Muslims." For their part, the Russians make a strong show of solidarity with the Afghan regime and blame Teheran and the U.S., China and Egypt for causing trouble. The ethnic Iranian peoples of Soviet Central Asia, all strictly orthodox Muslims, follow the events in Iran with more excitement than can please the Soviets.

Orthodox Islam, at home and abroad, sees the atheist-Marxism of the Khalq party as a threat, although no overt action has been taken against the mosques or against worship. Premier Amin says that Afghanistan is part of the Muslim world, "the only difference being that some countries make reference to religion, others do not."

But soft answers have not turned away Islamic wrath and in March 1979 Muslim zealots declared an official jihad. The Russians perhaps realized what they were up against when they heard the official jihad proclamation and a statement by a mullah that, "Our men are fighting with their rifles in one hand and the Koran in the other. They are fighting a pagan regime ... Jihad will mean the end of the Communists and the triumph of Islam, just as it has triumphed in Iran and Pakistan." Islam did not triumph immediately for in January 1980 the Soviet Union invaded Afghanistan on the pretext that the new puppet ruler, Babrik Karmal, had "invited" the Russians to defend his regime. Hundreds of thousands of Afghan hill tribesmen immediately became guerrillas and fought back against the Russian army. From the West's point of view Afghanistan is an interesting test for the ability of the Soviet Union to make an Islamic state into a genuine puppet state, that is, an entirely submissive one. The odds are heavily against this happening.

The Soviet leaders face an acute dilemma. They desperately want to convince foreign Muslims that the Soviet Union is friendly towards Islam but occasionally in their efforts to forge an empire their actions certainly appear anti-Islamic. For instance, in 1977 the Soviet Union shifted its support in Africa from Muslim Somalia to Christian Ethiopia. In their own Muslim republics of Uzbekistan, Tadzhikistan, Turkmenia, Kirghizia and Kazakhstan they have a bigger problem—the campaign to "liberate from religion" 50 million Muslims and thus bring Islam to an end within the Soviet borders. There are now only 500 working mosques compared with 24,000 before 1917, yet two of the five biggest cities in the Soviet Union are Muslim centers: Tashkent (1.8 million people) and Baku (1.55 million people). Only 30 Muslims a year are permitted to make the pilgrimage to Mecca as "representatives of Soviet Islam." A strictly limited number of copies of the Koran is available and there is only one Koranic school—in Uzbekistan. Despite their power, in this republic the Soviet leaders have not been able to eradicate the practice of the sale of brides.*

The Uzbeks are still so profoundly Islamic that they believe that one day the great eleventh-century conqueror Tamurlane will return to lead them against the infidel Russians. His body in its black onyx tomb in Samarkand has a powerful influence on Russian Muslims

If the turmoil in Turkey and Iran disturbs Western foreign ministries, it must equally disturb the Soviet foreign ministries. There is perhaps a reality here on which the democratic states and the communist states can agree: that Islam is a threat to them both. Islam's threat to the

---

*A virgin costs 500 roubles, 200 kilos of flour, 50 kilos of rice, two sheets and nine suits.

democratic West lies in its use of the oil weapon, its vast accumulation of money and gold in payment for oil, and its desire to impose a universal rule of Islam. The threat to the communist states is not so very different. For the moment they have adequate oil but Soviet planners know that within 10 years at most they will need Middle Eastern oil; they would not tolerate a refusal by the Islamic states to supply it. Again, to Islam the atheistic communist world is as much an "area of war" as is Christendom, especially since the Soviet Union's invasion of Islamic Afghanistan. The Russians also perceive the Muslim oil countries' ever increasing control over the world's economy as a threat.

The firmest common ground shared by the democracies and the communist states is that Islam spells instability and friction, which neither side can afford. It is not beyond possibility that Washington and Moscow, and their respective allies, will decide to neutralize Islam by joint action.

The complete reverse of such a course—an alliance between the West and Islam, no matter how desirable it might appear to Western politicans, would be unwise. The Muslim nations denounced the Soviet invasion of Afghanistan but they also warned the West not to overact. The government-controlled Saudi Arabian daily *Okaz* wrote that "communism is out to destroy the Muslims, their creed and their civilization"—but it has several times said the same of the West. The notion that the West and Islam are automatically allies because they have a common enemy has no meaning in the Islamic world. The old saying "An enemy of my enemy is my friend" has currency only *within* the Islamic world and even then is limited in application.

Those outside Islam are lumped together as *one* enemy, as Cairo's conservative Muslim magazine *Al Da'wah* made clear in April 1979: "The Muslims are coming, despite Jewish cunning, Christian hatred and the Communist storm."

In the long term Islam could also pose a threat even to China, which has a sizeable Muslim population—perhaps as many as 40 million—in the autonomous region of

Xinjiang, in the heart of Asia. A score of mosques flourish in Urumqi, the capital, though their survival is a matter of tolerance rather than encouragement. The Chinese permit the maintenance of Muslim "customs" but not really of Islam as a religion. To this end they allow special leave of absence from work for Muslims to observe Ramadan but pilgrimages to Mecca have been banned since the cultural revolution. Chinese families are strictly instructed not to allow their pigs to run in the streets so that Muslim sensibilities will not be offended. Despite this show of courtesy new copies of the Koran cannot be imported. Nevertheless, because Xinjiang is regarded as a frontier land the Chinese authorities are aware that outside influences can have "undesirable" effects and in the wake of the general Muslim awakening they watch their own Muslims closely.

18
OUT WITH THE DAGGER

Crusaders returning to Europe from Syria in the twelfth and thirteenth centuries brought with them the word "assassin," the name of an extremist Muslim sect, a branches of the Ismailis. Gradually the word became synonymous with murderer, though assassin was the stronger term. In their time the Assassins were a dangerous threat to all established order—religious, political and social. Through travelers' tales and legends, in the West the Assassins became notorious as fanatics and we still use *assassination* to describe a particular form of killing—that which has a political motive or a political victim. Possibly the world's first terrorists, the Assassins always killed by the dagger and they murdered many notable men, mostly Sunni leaders, in Syria and Persia. Their victims had been blacklisted as ungodly and as sinners against Islam. The murders were not opportunist killings but were carefully planned and carried out with a dedication and devotion to "the cause."

Seven centuries after the Crusaders startled Europe with the first stories of the Assassins the world is seeing Muslim assassins at work again. In the period since the end of World War II they have killed in every part of the Islamic world—and as far away from it as London and Paris. Frequently the assassins are Palestinians but most recently Iranians, encouraged by their ayatollahs, have joined the ranks of dedicated killers.

162

In May 1979 the Chief of Iran's central Islamic Revolutionary Court, Sheikh Khalkhali, said that anybody who killed the Shah, his family and aides in exile would be acting on orders of the court. He included the Shah's brother, Gholam Reza, his wife, Farah, and his last prime minister, Shahpour Bakhtiar. "Anybody who kills them," he said, "cannot be arrested by a foreign government as a terrorist. He will simply be carrying out the orders of the court." Khalkhali even warned the U.S. against giving shelter to the deposed royal family and, echoing his superior, Khomeini, ridiculed Western justice. "In the West a defense lawyer only delays the conviction of real criminals."

Khomeini and his Islamic courts probably have in mind the Koranic precept—"Sedition is more grievous than killing"—Sura 11:191—when they sentence to death and execute their pro-Shah captives. Since these men were held to be guilty of sedition or worse, then killing them was Koran-ordained. A fundamental principle of Islamic life is that necessity makes legal what would otherwise be not legal—a precept taken to heart by Muslim leaders who seize power. It is a simple mental step to rationalize "necessity."

Some of the Shah's followers were guilty of barbarous cruelty but the killing of hundreds of men formerly in some way connected with the regime was a form of legalized murder carried out principally for revenge. Some victims were found guilty of "insulting Allah's representative"—Khomeini—and of such imprecise crimes as "corruption on earth," the definition of corruption being left to the prejudices of the Islamic court. In Iraq the courts have gone even further than those in Iran; in May 1979 an Englishman resident in Baghdad was found guilty of forming a Bible class for espionage purposes.

Within Islam, the "dagger"—in the form of machine gun, bomb and hangman's rope—is well bloodied. Men— and sometimes women—are struck down with a frequency and ferocity which is only dimly perceived in the Western world. Assassination is an accepted means of political expression. Between 1948 and 1979 25 heads of state and prime ministers were murdered and another 20 ex-prime ministers or senior ex-ministers. One was killed in London. Numerous unsuccessful murder attempts were made on the lives of other leaders—including fourteen known attempts to kill King Hussein of Jordan. In the same 30-year period there were 22 inter-Muslim wars and civil wars and on 32 occasions between 1958 and 1979 Muslim states broke off relations with other Muslim states —apart from the mass Arab repudiation of Egypt in 1979. During the years 1968-79 26 foreign, mostly Western, diplomats were assassinated in Muslim countries. That Islam's dagger will be used and used again is not just a matter of speculation, the Lebanese War of 1975-6 alone proves that. Some other massacres are horrifying in their immensity. For instance, in March 1970 about 30,000 members of the El Ansar religious sect were killed on Aba Island in the Nile by the Sudanese army.*

Plots and counter-plots abound in Islam. The first phase of the Iranian revolution was scarcely over before emissaries of Khomeini were visiting Damascus to discuss ways of cooperating with the Syrians at the expense of Iraq, despite the fact that Syria and Iraq have declared themselves a "union." The Iranian-Syrian strategy is to stir up Shi'a opposition to the ruling Sunni clique in Baghdad. Khomeini wishes to weaken Iraq, a traditional rival of Iran, from within.

The extent to which the West is vulnerable to Islam's dagger needs to be carefully and coolly assessed. Understanding and sympathy are necessary, for much of the Islamic world is insecure, suffering simultaneously from a historical inferiority complex and an oilpower superiority complex.

Superficially studied, Islam as a *whole* would appear to have five possible courses in its relations with the rest of the world—always assuming that it does not tear itself apart with its schisms and conflicts.

> To fight a stubborn rearguard action in defense of
> its social/religious/political system.

---

*Report by Radio Amman, January 12, 1917. Egyptian estimates put the figure at "several thousand."

To go onto the offensive and make new conquests from *within* "enemy" countries by economic and propaganda means.

To reach a more or less formal state of détente with the West.

To compromise on an intellectual basis of give and take and tolerate.

To temporize and hope for better times in a future generation.

A sixth course—military conquest—appeals to some Muslims but practically nobody recognizes this as practicable in the foreseeable future. In reality, whatever a few individual nations might do, Islam as a whole can take only a few directions, for there is nothing in the Koran about détente, compromise or "intellect." Temporizing is not only permitted it is sometimes advised, but most Muslims feel they have temporized for far too long.

The most likely future for Islam internationally is that it will fight a rearguard action while weakening its "enemies" from within, as it has been doing since the early 1970s.

The French Islamic scholar, Maxine Rodinson believes that the Muslim world's future is one of struggles between social groups and between nations and that it may just be possible to make these struggles take the form of peaceful contests. But at a time when the Imams are powerful, and preaching that Communists, Christians and Jews are a danger to Islam, peaceful struggle and competitiveness seems remote. Much depends on the major leaders of Islamic states. Unfortunately, wise and tolerant men like Habib Bourguiba of Tunisia are rare. It was Bourguiba who said, "Each time that men by negotiation and goodwill succeed in finding an answer to the conflict of powerful national interests, the whole world from East to West should pause for a moment in silence, meditate on the lesson and draw from it fresh inspiration."*

*An article in *L'Express*, February 5, 1955.

Bourguiba might have been writing of the Israel-Egypt peace treaty nearly 25 years later, when he remained aloof from the general Arab denunciation of President Sadat. Sadat and Bourguiba, and Suharto of Indonesia, and to some extent Numeiri of the Sudan, are Islamic realists. In Sadat's case this must be partly because he was educated at a Christian school, where he learned something of compromise.

Among Islamic leaders, apart from the monarchs, several principal types are apparent. They are:

The politically active ayatollahs, sheikhs and mullahs.

The professional secular politicians who do not want an Islamic state—though some of them are good Muslims.

The "traditional-progressives" who want to build a "democratic" structure on the old religious bases.

The charismatic interventionists who passionately want to make Islam a force in the world.

The opportunists, ready to vary their policy according to circumstance.

Among the first group, the holy men who are ready to kill in God's name, the name of Ayatollah Khomeini is the best known. Either as individuals or as members of recognized political groupings—the very existence of which they themselves condemn—the religious men are among the most violent of Islamic leaders. Having dedicated themselves to the creation of the Islamic republic, these men are the most vehement advocates of a political pan-Islam and of jihad against unbelievers. They are rather like latter-day officials of the Spanish Inquisition, but they would go back far beyond it, to the days of Islam in the seventh century. Fanatics almost to a man, they are dangerous because they can incite the masses. They see themselves as reformers, although in reality they are destroying reforms. The ageing ayatollahs cannot be identified with modern Muslim nationalism; indeed, as fundamentalists they reject it, along with all the modernizing brought about by leaders such as Kemal Ataturk and Abdel Nasser.

The rigid nature of Khomeini's beliefs—and the dangerous extremism they pose—is easily seen in extracts from his book *Islamic Government,* a collection of lectures given in Iraq in 1970.

In our day... the government, authority and management over the people, as well as the collection and expenditure of revenues, has been entrusted to the religious experts. God will punish anyone who disputes their authority.

Government in Islam is not absolutist. It is constitutional—not, however, in the commonly understood sense of constitutionalism as represented in a parliamentary system, or in a system of popular assemblies. It is constitutional in the sense that those in power are bound by a group of conditions and principles made clear in the Koran and by the example of the Prophet Muhammad... Thus, Islamic government is a government of divine law. The difference between Islamic government and constitutional government—whether monarchical or republican —is this: In the latter system, the representatives of the people or those of the king legislate and make laws. Whereas, the actual authority to legislate belongs exclusively to God. No others, no matter who they may be, have the right to legislate, nor has any person the right to govern on any basis other than the authority that has been conferred by God.

Since Islamic Government is a government of law, it is the religious expert and no one else who should occupy himself with the affairs of government. It is he who should function in all those areas in which the Prophet functioned—neither adding nor diminishing from these in the slightest degree. He should implement the canonical punishments, just as the Prophet did, and he should rule according to God's revelation.

... There is no room for opinions or feelings in the system of Islamic government: rather, the Pro-

phet and the Imams and the people all follow the
wish of God and his laws.

We want a ruler who could cut off the hand of his
own son if he steals, and would flog and stone his
near relative if he fornicates.

The most outstanding of the second group, the professional politicians, was Muhammad Jinnah, the creator of
Pakistan; his manipulation and exploitation of the hopes
and fears of India's Muslims to bring about the state of
Pakistan is an example of pragmatic political skill at its
best—or worst. Jinnah himself was secular and non-
Islamic and he wanted that kind of state, but he worked
on religious Islamic sensibilities in order to get it. The
ill-fated Bhutto, more sophisticated but less astute than
Jinnah, tried the same ploy—and failed. He will be described in history as the man who invented the slogan
"Islamic socialism," a meaningless term if ever there was
one. Another professional politician is Bulent Eçevit of
Turkey, a realist frustrated by his inability to explain to
his people the benefits of education and of social cooperation. In Afghanistan, Nur Muhammad Taraki is also one
of the realist school who can see that the Afghans will be
better off as part of the 20th century world than holding
to the practices of ancient Islam, but many of his reforms
have been frustrated.

The third group of militant leaders, the "traditional-
progressives," can for the West be the most dangerous of
all; though short-term they are even more dangerous to
the present political leaders of Arab regimes. Professional
zealots, these men are more worldly wise than the ayatollahs. They know that their Islamic ideals can be reached
—and held—through political action and they use violence as a deliberate means to a desired end. Their
strength is in their group discipline and motivation. I have
always been struck by the similarity of their organization
with that of European communists—the same emphasis
on self-contained cells, the courier contact with other
cells, the policy of waiting and watching while being
ready to strike. The most obvious examples are the Muslim Brotherhood in the Arab world and Jamaat-i-Islami

in Pakistan. These two, again like communist parties, have strong cross-border links; if a Muslim Brother needs sanctuary he can find it in Pakistan.

The leaders are often depicted as coarse ruffians or fanatical terrorists. In fact, they are generally professional men or academics and sometimes poets and philosophers, and most of them have not personally committed a terrorist act. They have no need to, since they use their rank and file, who come mostly from the urban lower middle class. Ambitious but under-educated, jealous of their superiors, the men of this class can easily be incited to violent action from the crudity of a public demonstration to the finesse of a terrorist coup.

The traditionalists are such an obvious threat to national establishment that some prime ministers and presidents have outlawed them, thus depriving them of a living. Many have been imprisoned for long periods and some have been tortured. But, as in Communism, the cells survive and remain a constant threat to the government. They do this through their clandestine publications and through their modern approach to the power of publicity. Yet again like the Communists, they preach "democracy" without meaning it in the Western sense of the word. Islamic politics, the traditionalists say, would be democratic in that the leader would be elected. What they do not say is that this man would be nominated and would stand unopposed. They are equally silent about there being only one party.

They want not an Islamic state but an Islamic society. To the Western mind the two terms might appear to be virtually synonymous but there is a big difference between the Ayatollah Khomeini's state and the Muslim Brotherhood's society. The "progressives" accept and would use the Shira'a, the Koran, Hadith and Sunnah but onto them they would graft new legislation to cover the many aspects of modern life not even hinted at in the traditional sources.

The new laws would be drafted by a "council of righteous men," both clerical and lay. Their task would be to produce a wide range of laws in keeping with the spirit of the Shari'a and extending it give the modern

Muslim an answer to every problem in a complex world.

Some of the "progressives" I have met are idealists with pronounced ideas about social reform; but they are frightening idealists, since they want compulsory reform at almost any price. They are not prepared to discuss reforms with opposing groups nor will they compromise.

General Zia of Pakistan must be considered among the so-called progressives though in the fervor of his zealotry and his ignorance of political cause and effect he is more akin to Khomeini than to the Muslim Brotherhood.

Moammar Gaddafi is the principal charismatic leader. The late Mustafa Barzani, the Red Mullah of the Kurds, also fell into this category. King Hassan of Morocco would *like* to be regarded as charismatic and has worked hard to invest himself with charisma.*

From his revolutionary socialist standpoint, Gaddafi believes that his religion gives his revolution a moral base. He loathes the Saudis, who believe that their moral base comes from historical continuity. In 1974 Gaddafi declared, "We have solved the problem of democracy" but his democracy is the type which enabled him summarily to execute early in 1979 a group of young officers accused of plotting against him. He attacks the Communist states for exploiting individuals in their "class dictatorship" but he buys huge quantities of arms from the Soviets— enough to set himself up as the war-stores quartermaster for the whole of Islam.

As he interprets the Koran, Gaddafi believes he has the right to impose his philosophy on his African neighbors to the south. He is largely responsible for the violence and terror in Chad where Muslim Arabs are fighting Christian blacks and animists.

He provides much of the massive finance needed by the PLO and he supports the Moro National Liberation Front in the Philippines, the People's Crusaders in Iran,

---

*He has not gone as far as Egypt's King Farouk in the last years of his reign. Threatened by forces he could not control, Farouk produced a spurious genealogy tracing his ancestry back to the Prophet. When I interviewed Farouk in exile in Rome in 1956 he told me earnestly about his breeding and complained bitterly that in deposing him the Egyptians had committed apostasy. He had convinced himself that his lies were facts.

the IRA in Ireland and Black Muslim extremists in the U.S.A. He also sent troops to Uganda to support Idi Amin, who tried by brutal means to impose the Muslim faith on largely Christian Uganda. In May 1979 Gaddafi offered to train in Libya 1,000 terrorists of Joshua Nkomo's Patriotic Front to fight in Zimbabwe-Rhodesia against the elected Musorewa administration.

Gaddafi is said to be mad, but having interviewed him at length I doubt that he is in any way pathologically insane. Fanatical he certainly is, and he has profound ambitions to be the leader of the Islamic world; much of his nation's oil wealth is spent towards achieving this ambition. His interference in the affairs of other countries, in the name of jihad and "Islamic solidarity," is notorious. Today jihad can only be declared by individual states though Gaddafi and others would like to decree it for Islamic nations as a whole. An imperialist, Gaddafi has urged other Muslim leaders to join with him in a jihad to restore the great days of Islamic empire.

The opportunitists who make up the final group of leaders include Hafez Assad of Syria, General Hussein of Iraq and Said Barré of Somalia. They play East against West and are alternatively friends and then enemies of their neighbors. This is especially so in the case of Syria and Iraq who live in daggers-drawn suspicion of each other but at times manage to give the appearance of being allies.

All types of Muslim leaders have drawn the dagger and will do so again, and it is no consolation that mostly they do so to cut one another's throats; in an economically complex world third parties sometimes suffer more than the belligerents. In any case, virtually the entire world is vulnerable to the PLO and its hit teams, which at the one time had accepted contracts for the killing of the Shah and his family, President Sadat and King Hassan of Morocco. PLO terrorists are as indoctrinated as the original assassins and thoroughly imbued with the pleasures of the paradise waiting for those Islamic martyrs who die in combat against infidels. Not that the PLO gangs kill only infidels—many Muslims are among their victims. A gang killed Wasfi el-Tel, the Jordanian Prime

Minister, in Cairo in 1972—and one of them licked his blood.

Islam is at the mercy of its own institutionalized violence, and it faces other dangers, one of which was discerned by the great Orientalist Alfred Guillaume in a 1954 book on Islam.* "The old forces of reaction [may be] too strong for the new spirit of liberalism, armed as they are with shibboleths and anathemas which can arouse ignorant masses and terrorize men of vision. Only time can show which party will gain the upper hand." A quarter of a century later time had already shown that the spirit of liberalism was being strangled by old men brandishing old chains. Their solution to Islam's problems is a return to religious values but this cannot work indefinitely because it is rigid, legalistic, elitist and theocratic. These characteristics will intensify conflict and produce schisms within societies that have known little else in their modern existence.

But when a ruling group claims to be doing something in Allah's name while following Koranic precepts it becomes almost impossible for anybody to challenge this group without risking violence and bloodshed. Some Muslims, under the influence of socialist ideologies, might rebel against fundamentalist interpretations. These more enlightened Muslims see that the system presented to them as perfect is perfect only because they have made it apparently impregnable behind the walls of tradition. Should large numbers of Muslims become enlightened much strife will occur between them and the fundamentalists but in the end Islam will be breathing freely.

What a genuinely progressive Islamic nation could be is shown by Indonesia, which brought in a law in 1969 to the effect that Indonesia would not be a state for Socialists, Catholics, Protestants or Muslims. This reaffirmed the constitution, which makes no express mention of Islam, though the nation has four Islamic political parties.

A friend of mine, Dr. H. N. S. Mintaredja, for a long period a senior government minister, wrote a book on

*Islam, republished by Penguin, 1978.

Islam in Indonesia (1972) in which he urged Indonesian Muslims to show tolerance. "Let us, and especially the younger generation of Muslims, make a point of showing our religion to be good and without fault, through actions positive in nature and of benefit to all groups ... Does not the Prophet's attitude provide an example of great congeniality and tolerance towards other religions and their followers?"

Like many Indonesians, Dr. Mintaredja is critical of Arab Islam. "It is obvious that Arab nations which can appropriately be called Muslim countries are greatly lacking in vital spirit or élan, progressiveness and inspiration."

But Indonesia, at the far end of the Islamic arc, is relatively unimportant in world affairs and offers no threat. The West must regard more seriously the hostility which radiates from the heartlands of Islam. The prospects are bleak, for in the Islamic mind the West is to blame—for everything. National and personal difficulties have come from the "hostility, arrogance and corrupting influence" of the West. Though deeply divided, most Arab Muslims and many others agree on one thing—that the United States is ultimately responsible for the mess they find themselves in. This sweeping blame is unfair but hurt pride is best soothed by rationalization and the Arabs have developed the acceptable notion that the West, and the Americans in particular, because of many sinister and selfish motives, have kept the Arabs down, preventing them from acquiring the vital skills the West itself possesses.*

Since the West has "cheated" Islam of its destiny Islamic instinct is to want, even to demand, that history should recover from this lapse and return again to the true pattern of Islamic power. By wresting Iran from the Shah, by using oil power as a weapon to gain the respect of the West, by making war on Israel, by building 300 mosques in Britian, by having two million Muslims living

---

*A few Muslim writers, notably among them the Algerian Malek Bennabi, have admitted that the coming of Europe into the world of Islam enabled Muslims to escape from their decadence by breaking up their rigid social order and freeing them from belief in occult forces and fantasies.

in France, Muslims are more confident that they have put history back on an even keel and that Koranic navigation is once more on course.

The zealots of Islam believe that Christianity is in its failing phase. An Egyptian scholar who is also a traditionalist revolutionary told me, "This is the period of post-Christianity, and Judaism is no obstacle, except in the temporary stumbling block of Israel. So during the next twenty years we can make Islam supreme over the West."

Unfortunately, the West is led by the U.S., whose policy-makers appear to be ignorant of Islam, and unable to put any event into an historical context. Perhaps they know little Islamic history; certainly they know little of Muslim thinking, as they showed by hasty recognition and placation of their previous opponents, the Shah's enemies. This instant recognition was meant to win favor with Khomeini; in fact even he thought that the American *volte face* was dishonorable. The rapid shift of position was also unwise in that it forced the new Iranian administration to question just how firm American "recognition" would be to them. If recognition was meant to be a token of humility that too was wrong; humility is no more valued in Islam than compromise.

Muslims cannot tolerate shock without violent reaction but as the Middle East concept of time and history is slow moving, shock can last a long time and reaction to it can be delayed. Resurgent Islam is a reaction to the shock of 100–200 years of Western domination. It is also a reaction to the humiliation of the Muslim defeat in the 1967 Israeli-Arab war. Consciously and sub-consciously Muslims wish to retaliate in kind. They know from their religious teaching that Christians and Jews are inferior to Muslims and they will prove it. To the Muslim a man's self-respect depends primarily on the respect others show for him. To gain respect Muslims have resorted to force. This force is sometimes physical, as with terrorism. The Palestine Liberation Organization and its subsidiary terrorist groups have become highly paid enforcers for the Muslim world. Having found that their original aim to destroy Israel cannot be fulfilled they have turned to international terrorism as a way of life. Within weeks of Iran's successful revolution they had become Khomeini's secret police, carrying on where the infamous Savak had left off, and with the same methods, including torture. The PLO has carried out innumerable contracts in the Western world, many of them in no way connected with Israel. Certain Muslim leaders, unable to mount open military offensives, will increasingly use the PLO and its associated non-Muslim terrorist groups, to strike at the West.

But the principal *force*—apart from the insidious *influence* of propaganda—is that of oil sanctions, severe cuts in supplies and punitive price increases. But power does not lie only in the possession of vast amounts of oil; Western economies depend to a critical extent on the reinvestment of money paid for oil to the Muslim producers. The tremendous economic power which results from this confirms the Muslims' belief that Islam is the only true way, since Allah has given them the means to subdue the West, Christian and Jew alike.

Generally, as Peregrine Worsthorne summed up the situation (*Sunday Telegraph,* London, December 17, 1978) the West is facing a resurgent Islam with implacable motives "which transcend reason and encompass religious rage and revenge."

From such deep passions the dagger is drawn.

It helps to remember that to Islam all we non-Muslims live in Dar al-Harb, the area of mankind still unsubdued to Islam—the "house of war." As the men of al-Azhar have proclaimed—"Jihad will never end . . . it will last to the Day of Judgment."

This pursuit of power has reached a critical point, for Islamic countries are eager to acquire nuclear weapons. Egypt was the first to begin the drive towards a nuclear rocket capability in the early 1960s but this was thwarted by covert Israeli Intelligence action. More recently Iraq has begun work on its nuclear armament plans but, according to Western Intelligence sources, in 1979 Iraq was overtaken by Pakistan. Poverty-stricken Pakistan is in no position to finance a nuclear build-up, but it has wealthy backers—Saudi Arabia and Kuwait. It is safer for the

Arab states to develop a nuclear capacity by proxy than to alarm the West by doing so themselves. In time, with nuclear weapons reinforcing the "oil weapon" Islam might seek "domination and power and strength and might" even beyond the dreams of the early Muslims.

19

THE WORLD HELD HOSTAGE

Tensions and frictions within Islam are so intense that they generate violence with a speed and to a pitch not widely understood in the West until the events of 1979–80. In particular the Government-sponsored seizure of the American embassy in Teheran and the holding of American diplomats as hostages marked a new awareness of terrorism and the Islamic revolution. It also brought home to United States leaders, for the first time, the international implications of the revolution.

The subsequent Iranian rebuffs to the World Court, the United Nations Security council and to the UN Secretary-General personally may equally have shown the world at large that Islam will not compromise.

When Iranian students took over the embassy on November 4, 1979 they began a chain reaction of events which created an historical turning point. Their action was against international law, against diplomatic tradition, against human rights and against the United Nations Charter. It was also against the Koran; ironically Ayatollah Khomeini, in sanctioning the takeover, condoned the violation of Islam's age-old protection of foreign emissaries. The Koran forbids deliberately fomented violence, yet Khomeini was guilty of just that.

Khomeini's power is awesome, for he can make a

decision and have it acted on without the necessity of a formal statement or even of words. It is enough for him to wave his hand, twitch his eye, give a pained sigh or make a passing remark. In the summer of 1979, after glancing at a copy of the liberal newspaper *Ayandegan,* he murmured that he wished he did not have to read "this sort of thing." Next day mobs stormed the newspaper's offices, forcing it to cease publication.

The U.S. embassy seizure followed Khomeini's denunciation of "American imperialism" in admitting the Shah to the U.S. for medical treatment and his demand that he be returned to Iran for trial. Once again his storm-trooper students went into action, as Khomeini knew they would. The relationship between the ayatollah and the students is a form of mystical marriage, as one of his counsellors has said. He both absorbs and creates their values and demands. When the students issued a statement* which said "The U.S. does not seem to realize that it is fighting God," they were obviously quoting Khomeini.

Anti-Western and specifically anti-American feeling in Iran is neither surprising nor irrational, though it takes seemingly bizarre and irrational forms. That the deep anger at the Shah, and the U.S. which supported him, turned into fanaticism, is only to be expected among Shi'a people, who lead a passionate, activist religious life.

Americans saw a little of this passion in television films of the Ashura ceremony in Teheran, on the eve of the most important day of the month of mourning that begins the Muslim year. On this occasion hundreds of thousands of men paraded through Teheran's streets reciting verses from the Koran and flailing their backs with zanjira— small iron chains. Most marchers wore light shirts that soon became torn and bloodied by the blows, struck to the rhythm of muffled drums. In December 1979 the mullahs prevented the marchers from indulging in another Ashura ritual—slicing their shaven heads with scimitars. The mullahs feared that this would be "misunderstood" by Americans as evidence of a barbaric culture.

---

*In a broadcast picked up by the British Broadcasting Corporation, December 3, 1979.

The prolonged ordeal inflicted on the hostages was little less than barbaric despite the educated status of their captors. The ignorance of some students is frightening and sad—though understandable in the light of Muslim education. When journalists asked about evidence of spying by embassy staff one student said, "We have proof that they were in constant touch with Washington." Again, one of the most suspect hostages was the embassy code clerk. To be educated but not to know that all embassies, including Iranian ones, have codes, demonstrates abysmal ignorance. Most of the students are in their early twenties, with a strong almost Marxist sense of their own right. They are impatient of Western power structures and they are prepared to use any means to get their own way. Many are frustrated because, having gained qualifications, they cannot then find commensurate positions. One faction in the embassy episode was composed of seminarians from the theological college at Qum; many others were from the Teheran campuses. All are members of one of the three major political groups vying for position on the campuses of Iran's 53 universities and technical colleges. The Mujahedin, the largest and most influential group, consists of radical Islamic nationalists who support Khomeini as leader but fear his reactionary approach to Islam. Another leftist group, the Pishgam, is the student affiliate of the Marxist Feedayeen; the group's members are trained by the PLO. The far-right Hezb-Ollahis gives Khomeini unquestioning obedience and represents religious fundamentalism.

Evidence suggests that behind the mob scenes and chaos in Iran there is a master plan involving "student" terrorists around the world, financed largely by Libya and tied to Moscow. The Kremlin propaganda machine attributes the consequent disorder to fascists, U.S. agents and other "agents of imperialism." Intelligence agencies identified some of the "students" who carried out the U.S. embassy attack as K.G.B. agents, as well as several Palestinians, members of the specially trained PLO group assigned to Teheran to assist in the creation of a new secret police organization.

Soviet broadcasts to Iran encouraged the students in their anti-American, anti-West activities. When President Carter and Secretary of State Vance protested against the broadcasts, Moscow went through the motions of asking the students to release their hostages but passed the word that this request was not to be taken seriously. The Iranian students have always been satisfied that the Russians were backing them.

Whatever the power of the students and regardless of PLO and Soviet influence, the direct source of their inspiration is Khomeini. After the seizure of the embassy some of Washington's Middle East "experts" predicted that this flagrant violation of international custom would brand Khomeini as a pariah in the Muslim world. The experts were wrong. The only denunciations came from former Malaysian premier Tunka Abdul Rahman and President Sadat. Rahman said, "It is a shame that Iran, one of the progressive Muslim countries, has gone to the dogs." Sadat, having labeled Khomeini "a disgrace to Islam," became silent. Like other leaders he knows that Islamic holy firebrands can rouse the mobs to wild zealotry and he feared that Khomeini's success would inspire mad mullahs in Egypt.

Ned Temko of the *Christian Science Monitor* quotes a longtime associate of Khomeini as saying, "The ayatollah hates. In the West you put a premium on love. Islam, too, values love, but it is a Janus-faced faith, embracing also a burning hatred of Satan and of evil."

For Khomeini, his confrontation with the United States is his "one great battle against evil," a conflict between "oppressor and oppressed." After the embassy takeover Khomeini and his spokesmen vied with one another in finding insulting descriptions of the United States, as "the great Satan," "the blood-sucking center of predatory world capitalism," and "the evil world vampire," "the mother of corruption." Many mullahs in Iran and beyond sprinkle their preaching with the new words and phrases, which appeal enormously to their hearers. Even moderate Muslims, though they might deplore Khomeini's tactics, admire him for thumbing his nose at the West.

The *Guardian Weekly**   drew attention to perhaps the two most significant aspects of the Teheran U.S. embassy episode.

> The Ayatollah Khomeini claims to be acting in the name of his holy faith. In blindfolding hostages, abusing them and threatening them with death he is acting, so he says, in the name of God. That his defenseless victims are where they are under an agreement between his government and that of the U.S., granting them immunity from maltreatment, apparently makes no difference.

> Those thousands of eminent Muslim theologians who, by their silence, approve of what he is doing, should perhaps call attention to verses of the Koran where torment of the messenger and guest in the household is advocated and prescribed. [The *Guardian* is ironic; there are no such verses.]

Since every chapter, bar one, of the Koran, opens with the words "In the name of Allah, the Compassionate, the Merciful," the *Guardian* bitingly asked if the message of the Koran is that abuse of guests can be permitted here on earth because God will show compassion and mercy to him who commits it?

It was important to know, said the newspaper, whether the ayatollah was believed by Muslim theologians to be acting in accordance with the words of the Prophet, as he himself maintained. If he was, then Western perceptions of Islam and the value given to agreements would have to change. That such criticisms come from the *Guardian,* of all newspapers, is significant for it was foremost in its exposure of the misdeeds of the Shah.

What is at issue is simple good faith between countries when they promise protection for one another's envoys. As the Muslim world joined Khomeini (either by attacking American embassies or by a silence which gives consent) in saying that there is no such thing as good faith,

*London, December 9, 1979.

then the embassy crisis assumes a greater magnitude than most people thought.

Its magnitude was concisely expressed by Khomeini himself when he met 120 Pakistan Army officers at Qum. He made an inflammatory appeal: "I ask all Islamic nations, all Muslims and all Islamic armies, all Islamic military forces and heads of Islamic states to join our holy war."

To his own faithful he said, "This is not a struggle between the United States and Iran. It is a struggle between Islam and the infidel." He demonstrated the scope of the struggle in four significant incidents which followed the embassy takeover. On the first occasion the Pope asked Khomeini, in friendly and respectful terms, to act charitably and free the hostages. In his reply Khomeini accused the Pope of being a religious leader more interested in political expediency than in the teachings of Christ. The Vatican officials were affronted by the ayatollah's insult and exasperated by his hypocrisy. "It is blasphemy to decide that Jesus Christ would have sided with Carter," Khomeini announced in another venture into Christian thought.

The second example of conflict occurred in mid-December 1979, when the 15 judges of the World Court, from 15 countries including Poland and the Soviet Union, voted unanimously that Iran should free all the American hostages, clear the American compound and restore full diplomatic rights to the American officials. The Iranians boycotted the proceedings and ignored the court's verdict. This rebuff to the World Court was noted throughout the Islamic world, where the court may never again have any credibility.

The Security Council was also rebuffed when it voted unanimously that Iran should return the hostages. This was followed by the Iranians' hostility to the world's foremost diplomat, UN Secretary-General Kurt Waldheim, when he flew to Teheran. Ayatollah Khomeini refused to see him and Waldheim and his entourage could meet nobody in authority. After 48 hours he returned to New York humiliated and embarrassed, with the United Nations' stature considerably diminished. The UN five-man commission which visited Iran in February-March 1980 to investigate alleged crimes by the Shah was not permitted to see the American hostages.

In the embassy seizure the media learned once again that it must be extremely cautious in its dealings with terrorists. NBC made a deal with the Teheran students about interviewing one of the hostages; in effect, this meant agreeing to the students' terms. This was a dangerous precedent, since it could encourage all terrorists to believe that to get six minutes of prime air time for their propaganda they have only to take suitable hostages.

Americans' first reaction to the hostage crisis was outraged innocence—"What did we ever do to them?" The charge that they were imperialistic also confused them. The U.S. never colonized Islamic countries, as Britain and France did. The U.S. has no large Islamic minority and thus, unlike the Soviet Union, has no record of bitter internal relations with Muslims.

The root of the trouble is that since 1950 Islam's cultural encounter with the West has been more traumatic to Islam than colonialism—and the U.S. has led the West. Powerful, secular, materialist modernization has rolled into timeless Muslim villages. Muslim identity feels threatened by the vast machine of Western progress, which is profoundly tempting but at the same time horribly decadent, according to the disciplines of the Prophet.

Islam has difficulty in analyzing Western reaction to its violence. This was shown in an almost classic way by one of a series of Iranian foreign ministers, Sadegh Ghotzbadeh. In a television interview on December 27, 1979 Ghotzbadeh kept alluding to some sinister powers in the United States who were forcing the discussion away from the "real" issues and making it seem that the only issue was that of the hostages. The *Washington Post,* in a significant editorial,* stressed the "staggering magnitude" of Ghotzbadeh's misreading of the U.S. response to the acts of cowardice and criminality he and his friends pass off as Iranian "policy."

*December 29, 1979.

"There is something that Mr. Ghotzbadeh desperately needs to know," the *Post* editorial stated. "The hostages *are* the only issue." In logic and in humanity, perhaps, but Ghotzbadeh has a guiding maxim which ignores both —"We have the ideology to distinguish right from wrong, and we should not hesitate to tell misguided people, here and abroad, what is wrong with them."

Yet Ghotzbadeh was largely educated in the U.S.—at Georgetown University School of Foreign Affairs, where he was one of the best known dissident Iranian students in America. If he cannot comprehend the provocation of Islam and the Western response to it, how much more difficult for ayatollahs with seventh century minds.

American reactions to Iran and Islam have been restrained, all provocations considered, but the hostage crisis gave Americans a stereotype of the demented Muslim that only long years will change. This has been seen by Kemal Karpat, of the University of Wisconsin, who says, "Khomeini has done more harm to the Islamic image in one month than all the propaganda of the past 15 years."

Many Iranian Muslims believed by the end of 1979 that the American nation was reduced to that pitiful condition known to psychologists and other experts on terror—a childlike dependence on the goodwill or badwill of the terrorists, which produces great bursts of gratitude for favors and rewards and continued life.

With the United States in such dire trouble it was to be expected that its allies would speak out strongly against the seizure of the embassy hostages and would take retaliatory action, such as withholding goods and services. All America's allies should have responded at once and in strength of the president's appeal for a united front against the Iranian revolutionaries seeking to harness Islamic fervor in its campaign against the West. Instead, with the exception of Britain, they played safe by wringing their hands and doing nothing. It shows that Europe's politicians do not yet understand the danger of Islam and that they are as much at risk as the Americans.

With the embassy crisis at its height, Iran voted in a referendum on the new 175-article constitution. It was approved by 99% of Iranians—but this approval means nothing. The Revolutionary Council delayed distributing the documents until 14 days before the referendum, thus limiting the time for reading and debate. At several polling stations reporters for the state-owned television station found that nine out of ten people, many of them illiterate, had not read the constitution. Mullahs and armed revolutionary guards were posted at all polling stations, ostensibly to keep order; they were also able to keep a close watch on the open voting, since the ballot papers had two tabs—red slips for no votes and green ones, the color of Islam, for yes votes.

The fruits of revolution as expected by the masses are different from those planned by the mullahs, and the students have yet another vision. For the peasants revolution means land ownership and plenty to eat; the students expect sexual liberality and easy access to the good life with plenty of well-paid professional opportunities. For the mullahs revolution means the kind of theocratic power they have been seeking for centuries. It has also meant riches; throughout 1979 many mullahs smuggled cash and confiscated treasures abroad.

In December 1979 Muslim violence again reached into the Western world; Prince Shafik, a nephew of the Shah, was assassinated in Paris. As one of the few men capable of forming an effective opposition to the Khomeini regime, the prince was a prime target. The murder was organized by General Hossein Fardoust, close military adviser to Khomeini and commander of Savamba, the new Iranian secret police. General Farazian, deputy Savamba chief, and another general, Kaveh, then based in the Iranian embassy in Paris, were also involved.

The Ayatollah Khalkhali, responsible for revolutionary trials in Iran, announced that assassinations and judicial executions would continue "until all these dirty pawns of the decadent system have been purged."

In Iran itself assassination follows assassination. In December 1979 gunmen shot down Dr. Mohammad Moffateh, one of Khomeini's most influential followers, and his two bodyguards. The killings had all the hallmarks of Forghan, the terror group which considers all senior Islamic figures as legitimate targets. As Dean of Teheran

University's Theology Department and head of one of Teheran's revolutionary committees, Moffateh was a significant choice as a victim.

The divisions among the ayatollahs are deep and are yet another example of the hatreds within Islam. The differences between Ayatollah Khomeini and Ayatollah Shariat Madari have been well publicized. Madari is spiritual leader of the Muslim People's Republican Party which claims three million members of the province of Azerbaijan. When he expressed opposition to the rigged constitution, Khomeini supporters machine-gunned his home.

People in the West, comparing photographs of Shariat Madari with those of Khomeini, have described Madari as "benign," "a man with a sense of humor," "moderate" and "gentle." These labels are dangerously naïve and reflect a desperate wish on the part of the West to find a more acceptable figurehead than Khomeini. Undoubtedly Madari is more likeable than Khomeini but he is a product of the same teaching and the same life style; he has as much blind prejudice against the West and the United States but does not express it as violently as Khomeini.

One of the most disturbing developments of the Iranian revolution is that Palestine Liberation Organization elements have taken over the "dirty" jobs formerly handled by Savak. It was common knowledge in Iran in 1980 that people declared to be "enemies" or "traitors" were being tortured or killed by Palestinian punishment squads. Since the PLO leader, Yasser Arafat, is openly backed by Moscow, the presence of the Palestinians gives the Soviets a proxy foothold in Iran's power politics.

In an election in January 1980 Abolhassan Bani-Sadr, said to be a "moderate," was elected president of Iran; but even the president obeys the Ayatollah Khomeini and listens attentively to other ayatollahs as well.

Concurrently with revolution in Iran, violence has disfigured many parts of Islam, but nowhere more grotesquely than in Saudi Arabia where, in December 1979, nearly 500 fanatics attacked the mosque in Mecca. This was as great a sacrilege to devout Muslims as an attack on Jerusalem's Church of the Holy Sepulcher would be to

Christians or the Wailing Wall to Jews. Within Mecca power is shared between the royal governor, Prince Fawaz, and its spiritual head, Ab-dualaziz bin Bazz. The leaders of the obscure sect which attacked the shrine were well known to bin Bazz; he had secured clemency for them a few months earlier when they had been convicted of charges of sedition. These same men led the onslaught on the shrine.

Heavily armed and well trained by Yemenis and Cubans in Aden, the dissidents took up positions advised by the Yemeni tacticians. The timing was also professional—during the confusion of a well-attended dawn ceremony on the first day of a Muslim new century, 1400. In protracted fighting more than 300 insurgents were killed, including the leader of the group, Mohammad al-Quraishi, who called himself the Mahdi, and 170 taken prisoner. A theology student, al-Quraishi was influenced by Khomeini and financed by President Gaddafi of Libya. He and all others taken prisoner were beheaded.

Saudi Arabia is the target of a massive conspiracy to bring down the ruling families of the Gulf and place the oil fields within the grasp of forces opposed to the United States and the West. Since Saudi Arabia supplies the West with 22% of its oil imports the loss of this country as a source would cripple the U.S. and its allies. A necessary step is to destabilize the Saudi monarchy, hence the attack on the Mecca mosque. Other foreign-inspired uprisings have taken place at Medina and Al-Qatif. The Saudi rulers can control the situation until the National Guard turns against them, a real probability in the hands of the skilled Libyan, Iraqi and Iranian *agents provocateurs*. With the holy of holies no longer a safe haven the Muslim world is in ferment.

In Syria by 1980 terror was the predominant factor of public life. It had begun in June 1979 with Sunni Muslim fanatics killing members of the ruling Alawite sect at the rate of one a day. Since the Alawites make up only 10 per cent of Syria's population they felt bound to strike back harshly. Under a government reign of terror Syria's prisons were soon full of former senior politicians, diplomats and army officers who might provoke unrest. In December alone at least eight people were publicly executed in Damascus to deter the fanatics. The bitterness of inter-Muslim conflict in Syria was revealed by the Syrian ambassador to the United Nations, Hammoud El-Choufi, when he resigned from his post at the end of December 1979 in protest against Assad's police state with its "repression and corruption." In January 1980 he was second only to President Sadat on Assad's death list, but with civil war imminent, he expected his dangers to diminish.

The defeat of the moderate and pro-West Turkish premier Bulent Eçevit in October 1979 and the coming to power of Suleyman Demirel must result in even more violence. Politicians are increasingly Islam-conscious and terrorists more violently anti-West. Outrages such as the killing of four Americans by Turkish leftists in Istanbul on December 18, 1979 are commonplace.

In common with Iran, Iraq and Syria, Turkey has increasingly serious problems with its Kurdish community, which occupies a good third of the entire country and is under martial law. All the many Kurdish groups, though differing wildly on aims, means and beliefs, are openly secessionist. They want nothing less than a full-fledged Kurdish state. The Turkish Kurds, well to the left of their Iraqi and Iranian brethren, seek the transformation of Kurdish society along radical Marxist-Leninist lines. They are, they say, preparing for a popular liberation war. There has been a great influx of arms into eastern Turkey since 1977; nowadays families insist on a Kalashnikov rifle as part of the bride-price.

Turkish Kurds insist, far more than others, on their pan-Kurdism. Because of their numerical strength, geographical spread, historical experience and their conviction that it is futile to seek the patronage of neighboring states, they believe that it is their destiny to shoulder the main burden of the struggle. Thus Eastern or Kurdish Turkey has become the crossroads for an illicit traffic in Kurdish agents and refugees, as well as arms, that embraces all Kurdistan. Attempts to keep them divided into four national groups—with watchtowers along the Iraqi and Iranian frontiers and minefields along the Syrian one—are unavailing.

Despite all attempts to stop it, the Kurdish Democratic Part of Iraq held its eighth congress in December, though in the comparative safety of west Iran. Even there the delegates feared that the Iraqi president, Saddam Hussein, would send his air force to wipe them out. Hussein has carried out mass deportations, razed hundreds of villages in a security belt along the Turkish and Iranian frontiers, Arabized oil-rich Kirkuk, destroyed vegetation and poisoned the wells, and has imprisoned, tortured and executed Kurds by the thousands.

Even more critically for the West, many competing interests are seeking to overthrow the conservative monarchies of the Arab Gulf and to push the Iranian revolution further but, as always in Islam, they are divided by murderous enmities. Iraq, which aspires to be the leading power in the Gulf, is in a state of undeclared war with Iran and—despite cordial relations with Moscow—is feuding with Soviet-controlled South Yemen and with Syria.

The spillover from Iran makes American installations and personnel vulnerable to mob attack throughout the Muslim world.* This was demonstrated in December 1979 by the assaults on U.S. embassies in Libya (Tripoli), Pakistan (Islamabad), Bangladesh (Dacca) and Kuwait. In Islamabad a mob not only burned the embassy but killed two American servicemen; the Ayatollah Khomeini's reaction, according to *Time*'s report (January 7, 1980) was "great joy." In Tripoli the demonstrators, rounded up by official *provocateurs* and spurred on by pro-Khomeini slogans from sound trucks, fired the embassy, which was badly damaged.

In Kuwait and Bahrein, ruled by Sunni families related by blood and religion to the Saudi royal house, Khomeini agents encourage many demonstrations and riots by local Shi'a people demanding Islamic republics tied to Iran.

*The State Department lists 254 "significant" terrorist attacks against U.S. diplomatic installations or individuals in the period 1970–1980: the great majority were committed by Muslims.

There are substantial Shi'a minorities in the Gulf States, Lebanon and Turkey and here too Khomeini's followers are active in urging the Shi'a people to join in an uprising against Western influence; this nearly always means *American* influence.

Anti-American propaganda is crude but effective. "Blacks are still lynched in the United States, without trail, by ordinary people," the English-language *Teheran Times* stated on January 7, 1980. As Iranians have been told, in the U.S. blacks battle whites, women battle men, rich battle poor. Writing from Teheran in March 1980, *Christian Science Monitor* correspondent Ned Temko observed that in the Iranian view, "Atop a corrupt American power pyramid sits a president soon to be toppled by an outraged oppressed people sympathetic to Iran's grievances against Washington."

Just as the Americans and other Western peoples tried to build strong links between themselves and Muslims, so the Soviet Union has tried by other means to tie Islamic republics to itself. In Aden, by effacing all religion, the Russians dominate the South Yemenis. But the Iranian revolution poses as great a threat to the Soviet as it does to U.S. interests. Islamic fundamentalism is anathema to communism but Khomeini and his faction are religiously akin to the Muslims of Soviet Central Asia. On the other hand the Soviet National Security Council has assessed that anarchy in Iran could lead to its takeover by radical leftists favoring the Soviet Union.

While the United States was preoccupied with the Islamic revolution and trying to make friends with the Iranians—before the embassy seizure—the Soviet Union was increasing its influence in Afghanistan. The puppet ruler, President Taraki, visited Moscow on his way back from the non-aligned nations summit meeting in Havana. Here he was embraced by President Brezhnev, who nevertheless told him he was not making enough progress in overcoming resistance to the pro-Soviet regime. Three days later, in Kabul, Taraki was killed in a shoot-out in the People's (Presidential) Palace and Prime Minister Hafizullah Amin took over as president. After a sweeping purge of army officers and politicians, Amin embarked on his own campaign, with Russian help, to crush the rebel tribesmen.

When the Teheran embassy crisis had absorbed American attention, emotion and energy, the Russians saw their opportunity to be even more forceful. As Amin had not been able to secure Afghanistan totally for the Soviet Union, the Russians arranged for his execution, late in December, and installed Babrik Karmal as puppet ruler. This was immediately followed by an invasion—though the cover story was that first Amin and then Karmal had asked the Russians for help in crushing the rebellion.

The Islamic world was angered by the Soviet invasion and for a time the Teheran mobs demonstrated outside the Soviet embassy. However great the Islamic anger, and whatever the sanctions imposed by the United States and its allies, the Russians have demonstrated to Islam that they are neither afraid to quell Muslim uprisings nor perturbed about offending the religious sensibilities of Islam. At one stroke the Soviet Union has given itself another 1,000 miles of border along which to threaten the West; it is significantly closer to the Indian Ocean and the Middle East oilfields. By moving through Iran, virtually defenseless because of internal chaos, the Soviet Union could link up with its Syrian and Iraqi allies; by cutting through Pakistan they would reach the long-coveted Indian Ocean. Poverty-stricken and landlocked, Afghanistan is not desirable in itself but is the route to the great prize of the Middle East—vast, rich and sparsely populated Saudi Arabia, with its enormous oil reserves.

The United States therefore finds itself dealing with two enemies in one area at the same time—Militant Islam and Opportunist Communism. The two have many differences but one important thing in common: Both respect insistent, consistent firmness. Never has there been such a need for the West to show its strength. Islam now has great power and a policy—one part of which is humiliation of the West. The United States also obviously has power but since the Vietnam trauma its policy has been not to use that power. Non-use of power is a meaningless concept to Muslims and is seen only as a weakness.

In the early days of the Iranian Revolution former U.S.

Ambassador to the United Nations, Andrew Young, nominated the Ayatollah Khomeini for sainthood. On January 7, 1980 *Time* Magazine declared the ayatollah its "Man of the Year"—"the one who has done the most to change the news, for better or for worse."

Despite the public anger at *Time*'s nomination, perhaps the free world owes it to the Iranian crisis that its eyes are being opened to the nature of appeasement—that disease whose paralyzing virus infects attitudes towards political violence, terrorism, intimidation, harassment and political bargaining.

The Islamic revolution might be difficult to comprehend but for the West two facts stand out with singular clarity. One is that all the nations which depend on Muslim oil are held hostage to blackmail and are in a subservient state. The other fact is that now we know it.

SPELLING AND GLOSSARY

For the sake of simplicity I spell Arabic words and names as they were commonly used in leading English-language newspapers and journals. Hence, I use Koran rather than Qur'an and President Nasser (Nasir). I prefer Muslim to the equally used Moslem and Muhammad to Mohammad mainly because there is no letter 'o' in the Arabic alphabet. I have omitted most of the many diacritical marks such as accents and apostrophes which appear in transliterated Arabic. In general, I have tried to use the method of the *Shorter Encyclopaedia of Islam* (edited by H. A. R. Gibb and J. H. Kramers, Leiden: E. J. Brill, 1953).

'Abd (slave) Common in names—Abdullah.
Caliph (successor) The representative of God on earth and therefore the successor of the Prophet Muhammad. The title was first held by Arab and then by Ottoman rulers until the final overthrow of the Ottoman Caliphate after World War I.
Dar al-Harb The areas of mankind still unsubdued to Islam; the house of war.
Dar al-Islam The house of Islam, the actual realm of the Muslim faith in which Islam is in full political and religious control.

dhimmi   A non-Muslim living under a 'covenant' (*dhimma*) with special obligations to a Muslim government. A *dhimmi* is a second-class citizen who buys protection by paying a special tax.

hadith (communication or narrative)   The body of verbal *or* written traditions concerning the words and deeds of the Prophet Muhammad and his companions. Also, a single one of these traditions.

Hajj or Hadjdj   The pilgrimage to Mecca in the sacred month.

hegira or hidjra (breaking of relations or emigration)   The Prophet Muhammad's flight from Mecca to Medina in AD 622 is the date from which the Muslim era is counted.

imam   The temporal and spiritual ruler of Islam; a title of the Caliph. Also, a leader in prayer at mosques.

Islam   The act of surrendering oneself to Allah; literally the verb form of *islam* means to deliver over in sound condition. The common definition of *islam* is submission.

jihad or djihad   Muslim holy war against unbelievers whether pagan, Christian or Jew. Holy war is a duty of Muslims in general.

Kaba (cube)   The most important place of worship in Mecca.

Koran (reading or recitation)   The holy book of Islam, revealed by the angel Gabriel to Muhammad.

mahdi (guided one)   Name taken by various Islamic leaders who claimed divine enlightenment.

mudjahidun (sing. mudjahid; fighters for the faith)   Originally, the fighters in holy wars, in contemporary Middle East Islam especially Iran, nationalist guerrillas.

mufti   A qualified 'lawyer' able to give a legal opinion on the Shari'a; a person of considerable rank.

Muslim   Legalistically a Muslim, a follower of Islam, is one who says, 'I witness that there is no Allah but Allah, and Muhammad is the messenger of Allah.'

mutawwi   The official who ensures moral and religious obedience to Islam.

Ramadan   The ninth month of the Muslim lunar calendar in which the Koran was first revealed to Muhammad; observed by fasting and abstinence during daylight hours.

Shari'a (clear path)   The law of Islam.

Shi'a or Shi'ite (partisan)   A follower of the Muslim sect which rejects the first three Caliphs and the authority of the sunna. Shi'as say that Ali should have become caliph on Muhammad's death.

Sufi   A follower of a system of Islamic contemplative life.

sunna or sunnah (custom, usage or statute)   The orthodox code of Islamic practice transmitted through Muhammad's immediate successors.

sura   A chapter of the Koran.

ulama (pl. of alim)   Theologians who rule on important religious and political matters.

umma   The Islamic community of believers.

Zakat   Originally not so much a tax as an alms-giving. By giving alms a Muslim is purified.

FURTHER READING

Books recommended for further reading on certain aspects of Islamic life. All were in print in 1979.
General introduction to Islam Perhaps the best book is *Islam* by Kenneth Cragg, Dickenson Publishing Co., Encino, California. The author calls his book 'no more than an interpretation' but it is a clear and scholarly exposition within 145 pages. Alfred Guillaume's *Islam,* first published 1954 and reprinted several times by Penguin, is also useful. H. A. R. Gibb's *Islam,* published in 1949 and available in an Oxford University Press paperback, covers much the same ground.

ARABS *The Arabs,* Thomas Kiernan, Little, Brown & Co., 1975, 550pp. An authoritative firsthand account of the history, character and aspirations of the Arabs.

ASSASSINS *The Assassins,* Bernard Lewis, Weidenfeld and Nicolson, 1972. An interesting historical account.

CHRISTIANS *Christians in the Arab East, A Political Study,* Robert Duncan Betts, John Knox Press, Atlanta, 1975. Thorough analysis of the dilemma of Arab Christians.

CONFESSION *Letters on Islam,* Mohammed Fadel Jamali, World of Islam Festival Trust, 1978. (Originally O.U.P.) An Iraqi political prisoner writes to his son.

CURRENT AFFAIRS *Arabia Without Sultans,* Fred Halliday, Pelican, 1979, 528pp. A book with 'an anticapitalist approach' which attempts to provide a comprehensive analysis of the contemporary Arabian peninsula.

ECONOMICS *Islam and Capitalism,* by Maxime Rodinson, Penguin, 1977. An excellent, detailed account of Muslim economic practice and its inter-action with capitalism in modern times. Rodinson points out that Islam is already largely capitalistic.

EGYPT *Islam in Egypt Today,* Morroe Berger, Cambridge University Press, 1970. The organization and behavior of popular religious groups and the increasing effort of the government to control them.

ISLAMIC SOCIETY *The Social Structure of Islam,* Reuben Levy, Cambridge University Press, 1962. Covers family, jurisprudence, moral sentiments, military organization—to 1955.

ISLAMIC WRITING One of several useful books is *The Islamic World,* ed. McNeill and Waldman, Oxford University Press, 1973, 468pp. The book has examples of poetry, prose and oratory covering 1400 years.

THE KORAN For English-language readers the best versions are *The Koran,* translated by N. J. Dawood, Penguin, 1971, and *The Koran Interpreted,* Arthur J. Arberry, Oxford University Press, reprinted 1972.

LEBANESE CIVIL WAR *The Lebanese War,* Harald Vocke, C. Hurst & Co., 1978. Shows how religious passions became uncontrollable.

MUSLIMS IN THEIR UNGUARDED MOMENTS Dr. Ian Young's *The Private Life of Islam,* Allen Lane, 1974, cannot be too highly recommended. The book concerns Algeria.

MUSLIM THOUGHT *The Arab Mind,* Raphael Patai, Charles Scribner's Sons, 1973.
Arabic Thought in the Liberal Age 1798–1939, Albert Hourani, Oxford University Press, 1970.
The Muslim Mind, Charis Waddy, Longman, 1976—a useful anthology.

POLITICS *Political and Social Thought in the Contemporary Middle East,* Kemal Karpat, Praeger, 1968.

REFERENCE *Shorter Encyclopaedia of Islam,* 671pp., ed. Gibb and Kramers, E. J. Brill, Leiden, Holland.

Rhetoric and Reality: *The Arab Mind,* John Laffin, Taplinger, 1975.

SEXUAL LIFE *The Cradle of Erotica,* Edwardes and Masters, Odyssey Press, 1970. Frank and frightening. See also Young.

SLAVERY IN ISLAM *Slavery and Muslim Society in Africa,* Allan and Humphrey Fisher, C. Hurst & Co., 1970. *The Arabs as Slavers,* John Laffin in *Case Studies on Human Rights and Fundamental Freedoms,* vol. 4, Foundation for the Study of Plural Societies, The Hague, 1976.

TERRORISM *Fedayeen,* John Laffin, Free Press, 1973.

WOMEN *Middle Eastern Muslim Women Speak,* ed. Elizabeth Warnock Fernea and Basima Qattan Bezirgan, University of Texas Press, Austin and London. A splendid book of selections and excerpts from many parts of the Middle East. See also Young and Levy.

INDEX

ABOUT THE AUTHOR

JOHN LAFFIN is one of the best-known
writers on the Middle East and has
travelled widely in the Islamic world. His
books, which number eighty, include
Middle East Journey, Fedayeen (*The
Arab-Israeli Dilemma*), *The Arab Mind*
and *The Israeli Mind*. He is also a regular
contributor to the international press and
to world encyclopedias.

The Inquisitive Mind

Bantam/Britannica Books were created for those with a desire to learn. Compacted from the vast Britannica files, each book gives an indepth treatment of a particular facet of science, world events, or politics. These accessible, introductory volumes are ideal for the student and for the intellectually curious who want to know more about the world around them.

☐	12486	**THE ARABS: People and Power**	$2.50
☐	12487	**DISASTER: When Nature Strikes Back**	$2.50
☐	12488	**THE OCEAN: Mankind's Last Frontier**	$2.50
☐	12485	**THE U. S. GOVERNMENT: How and Why It Works**	$2.50
☐	13106	**CATASTROPHE: When Man Loses Control**	$2.50
☐	13105	**ENERGY: The Fuel of Life**	$2.50
☐	13107	**HOW THINGS WORK: Aerosols to Zippers**	$2.50
☐	13108	**LAW IN AMERICA: How and Why It Works**	$2.50

Buy them at your local bookstore or use this handy coupon for ordering:

Bantam Books, Inc., Dept. BN, 414 East Golf Road, Des Plaines, Ill. 60016

Please send me the books I have checked above. I am enclosing $_____ (please add $1.00 to cover postage and handling). Send check or money order —no cash or C.O.D.'s please.

Mr/Mrs/Miss_____

Address_____

City _____ State/Zip _____

BN—1/81

Please allow four to six weeks for delivery. This offer expires 7/81.

Bring out the books that bring in the issues.

Bantam Book Catalog

Here's your up-to-the-minute listing of over 1,400 titles by your favorite authors.

This illustrated, large format catalog gives a description of each title. For your convenience, it is divided into categories in fiction and non-fiction—gothics, science fiction, westerns, mysteries, cookbooks, mysticism and occult, biographies, history, family living, health, psychology, art.

So don't delay—take advantage of this special opportunity to increase your reading pleasure.

Just send us your name and address and 50¢ (to help defray postage and handling costs).